大学入試　レベル別英語長文問題
Solution 最新テーマ編1　スタンダードレベル

別冊問題　もくじ

JN106721

次の英文を読み、下の問い（ **問1** ～ **問5** ）の［　　］に入る最も適切な
ものを、それぞれ下の①～④のうちから１つずつ選び、解答しなさい。

A Bright Future

The sunlight that reaches Earth in one hour has as much energy
as all the power that people use in a year. But how can we get this
energy and use it on earth?

5　'Solar' means 'coming from the sun', so when you use sunlight to
make things hot, it is called solar thermal power. Many buildings
use materials like glass and plastic to catch sunlight and warm the
building. In Africa, people use solar cookers. When light hits the
surface of the cooker, it is reflected into the middle. The middle
10　becomes hot enough to heat water or cook food. In countries like
Turkey and China, people put solar water heaters on their roofs.
These are metal and glass boxes with water pipes in them. The glass
catches heat and the metal reflects sunlight onto the water pipes,
which carry the hot water down into the houses.

15　We can use sunlight to make electricity too, with devices called
solar cells, which are made of silicon. When sunlight hits the silicon,
particles inside it move, and this makes electricity. One solar cell
does not produce much power, so we put the cells together to make
big solar panels.

20　At the moment, the best solar cells can only use about 25 percent
of the sunlight that hits them, and they are an expensive way to

produce electricity. But people are inventing better and cheaper solar cells all the time. In the future, we will use them to do more and more things. You can already buy solar lights, solar radios, and
25 small solar panels for things like computers and phones.

We can use solar power to travel too. In July 2010, Andre Borschberg flew a solar plane called Solar Impulse for 26 hours before he stopped. Power for the four engines came from 12,000 solar cells on the wings of the plane. It was able to fly at night because of
30 batteries inside the plane which kept solar energy. There are also solar boats, and in the future, there may even be solar buses and trains. Moreover, every two years, in the World Solar Challenge, cars that are powered by solar energy travel over 3,000 kilometers in Australia. The fastest cars can reach speeds of 100 kilometers per
35 hour!

問1 According to the passage, solar thermal power [   ].
  ① is used to catch sunlight
  ② is heating things with sunlight
  ③ means 'coming from the sun'
  ④ catches sunlight like glass and plastic

問2 What is **NOT** given as an example of solar thermal power?
  [   ]
  ① Solar lights.   ② Solar cookers.
  ③ Solar water heaters.   ④ Building heating.

1 環境
2 社会
3 環境
4 健康
5 IT・テクノロジー
6 医学
7 環境
8 IT・テクノロジー
9 教育
10 社会

問3 According to the passage, what is true about solar cells?
[   ]
① They use most of the sunlight that hits them.
② They are inexpensive.
③ They make electricity through the movement of particles.
④ They are used for making hot water.

問4 According to the passage, what forms of transport use solar power now? [   ]
① Cars, trains, and boats.
② Trains, buses, and airplanes.
③ Airplanes, cars, and boats.
④ Boats, cars, and buses.

問5 What is the best summary of the passage? [   ]
① People should use more solar power.
② Solar power has many applications.
③ Solar power is getting cheaper.
④ Solar planes are amazing.

次の英文を読んで、各問いに答えなさい。

Identity theft is a growing problem for anyone who goes online. People used to worry about this crime only after their purse or wallet was stolen, but today an increasing number of people are victims of online identity theft. This happens when someone is tricked into downloading an unwanted program from a website or opening a file attached to an email. By doing so, a person may (ア) install "spyware," a computer program that can access his or her address book, bank account information, credit card numbers, user names and passwords.

The spyware secretly reports personal information back to the criminal hackers. They can then use information to illegally withdraw money from (イ), get credit card numbers, or create Internet accounts in someone's name. Information may even be sold to others who want to use it for illegal purposes.

Criminal hackers also sometimes use computer attachments to break into the websites of large companies. Then they steal the credit card information of the customers. (ウ)These attacks can come from anywhere in the world. In 2011, a major Japanese electronics company reported that information was stolen through the company's online services. The hackers got the user names, passwords and birth dates of 100 million users. In 2013, hackers stole the credit card information of 40 million users of a large

American department store chain. That same year, a Japanese Internet company said that information of 22 million customers might have been stolen. Now a great number of companies are （　エ　） of establishing more reliable security systems. Recently, in 2017, hundreds of thousands of computer users in over 150 countries lost access to their data because of the "WannaCry virus."

Still, there are things that people can do to protect themselves. When using a computer, it is a good idea not to open any emails sent from unknown people. It is also important to delete spam messages right away and never open junk email. One should avoid downloading software from websites you cannot trust, and everyone should have the most recent updates for their operating systems. When using a public computer, it pays to be extra careful. If you discover a company you do business with has been hacked, the best idea is to change your user name and password immediately. Also, watch all credit card activity closely and report anything unusual to the card company.

（注）
theft：窃盗　　spam：スパム、迷惑メール

問1 空所（　ア　）を満たすのに最も適切なものを、A～Dのうちから1つ選べ。

A　strongly　　　　　B　accidentally
C　severely　　　　　D　closely

問2 空所（　イ　）を満たすのに最も適切なものを、A ～ Dのうちから１つ選べ。

A　bank accounts　　　　　B　criminal hackers
C　electronics companies　　D　computers

問3 下線部（ウ）"These attacks can come from anywhere in the world."の意味に最も近いものを、A ～ Dのうちから１つ選べ。

A　Most of the danger to computers is in Japan or America.
B　The hackers work in many countries.
C　The world's customers are attacking.
D　People use computers to attack the world.

問4 空所（　エ　）を満たすのに最も適切なものを、A ～ Dのうちから１つ選べ。

A　in need　　　　　　　B　inside
C　in truth　　　　　　 D　in trouble

問5 次の書き出しに続く最も適切なものを、A ～ Dのうちから１つ選べ。
The author believes that（　　　　）.

A　computers are too risky to use these days
B　people should have many credit cards
C　downloading spyware protects computers
D　people should be careful when opening emails

問6 本文の内容に合致するものを、A ～ Dのうちから１つ選べ。

A　オンラインでの個人情報の盗難は、メールの添付ファイルを開くことによって発生することはない。
B　ハッカーは盗んだ情報を利用してクレジットカード番号を盗んだり、他人名義のインターネットアカウントを作ったりする。
C　小売業を含む色々な業界で個人情報の盗難は相次いでいるが、政府が厳しい対策を取れば解決は可能である。
D　取引業者のパソコンがハッキングされたと知ったら、すぐにクレジットカードを解約し、その旨を相手に伝える。

制限時間25分／400 words／解答：本冊 p.38

次の英文を読み、以下の問い（ 問1 〜 問6 ）の（　　）に入る最も適切なものを、イ〜ニからそれぞれ１つずつ選びなさい。また、 問7 は直接記入しなさい。

Here's How Much Plastic Trash[1] is Littering[2] the Earth

(1) Mass production of plastics, which began just six decades ago, has increased so rapidly that it has created 8.3 billion metric tons[3] — most of it in disposable[4] products that end up as trash. Even the scientists who set out to conduct the world's first calculation of how much plastic has been produced, disposed, burned or put in landfills[5], were surprised by the size of the numbers. "We all knew there was a rapid and extreme increase in plastic production from 1950 until now, but actually quantifying[6] the number for all plastic ever made was quite shocking," says Jenna Jambeck, an environmental (あ in、い who、う engineer、え specializes、お plastic、か studying) waste in the oceans.

(2) The study was launched two years ago as scientists tried to measure the huge amount of plastic that ends up in the seas and the harm it is causing to birds, marine animals, and fish. The prediction that by mid-century, the oceans will contain more plastic waste than fish has become one of the most-quoted statistics and a rallying cry[7] to do something about it. The new study, published in the journal Science Advances, is the first global analysis of all plastics ever made — and their fate. Of the 8.3 billion metric tons that has been

produced, 6.3 billion metric tons has become plastic waste. Of that, only nine percent has been recycled. The vast majority — 79 percent — is accumulating[8] in landfills or ending up in the natural environment as waste.

(3) Roland Geyer, the study's lead author, says the team of scientists are trying to create a foundation for better managing plastic products. "You can't manage what you don't measure," he says. "It's not just that we make a lot, it's that we also make more, year after year." Half the resins[9] and fibers used in plastics were produced in the last 13 years, the study found. The rapid growth of plastic manufacturing, which so far has doubled approximately every 15 years, has outpaced[10] nearly every other artificial material. And, it is unlike virtually every other material. Half of all steel produced, for example, is used in construction, with a decades-long lifespan. Plastic takes more than 400 years to degrade[11], so most of it still exists in some form. Half of all plastic manufactured becomes trash in less than a year, the study found.

注：

1 trash　くず、がらくた
2 litter　汚す
3 metric ton　メートルトン（重量の単位：＝1,000kg）
4 disposable　使い捨ての
5 landfill　埋立地、ごみ処理場
6 quantify　量を計る
7 rallying cry　スローガン、標語
8 accumulate　積もる、集まる
9 resin　樹脂
10 outpace　追い越す
11 degrade　分解する

1 環境
2 社会
3 環境
4 健康
5 Ｉ・Ｔ・テクノロジー
6 医学
7 環境
8 Ｉ・Ｔ・テクノロジー
9 教育
10 社会

問1 According to paragraph (1), plastic production has (　　　).

イ　continued slowly　　　　　ロ　speeded up
ハ　continued to decrease　　　ニ　remained the same

問2 According to paragraph (1), the scientists were shocked because the amount of plastic was (　　　).

イ　so large　　　　ロ　difficult to locate
ハ　so varied　　　ニ　difficult to calculate

問3 According to paragraph (2), by 2050 (　　　).

イ　more plastic will be in the oceans than fish
ロ　fish consumption will decrease
ハ　less plastic will be in the oceans
ニ　plastic use will decrease

問4 According to paragraph (2), approximately 570 million metric tons of plastic has been (　　　).

イ　disposed of　　　ロ　burned
ハ　recycled　　　　ニ　buried

問5 According to paragraph (3), every 15 years the amount of (　　　) doubles.

イ　plastic technology　　　ロ　plastic produced
ハ　plastic pollution　　　　ニ　plastic recycled

問6 本文の意味と合うようにパラグラフ (1) 中の括弧内の単語を並べ替えて、英文を完成させなさい。そして 2 番目と 5 番目にくる最も適切なものの組み合わせをイ～ニから選んで記号で答えなさい。

（　　　）

イ　2番目「あ」、　　5番目「え」
ロ　2番目「い」、　　5番目「お」
ハ　2番目「い」、　　5番目「か」
ニ　2番目「え」、　　5番目「お」

問7 パラグラフ（3）中の下線部を日本語に訳しなさい。

1 環境

2 社会

3 環境

4 健康

5 I・T・テクノロジー

6 医学

7 環境

8 I・T・テクノロジー

9 教育

10 社会

制限時間20分／360 words／解答：本冊p.48

次の英文を読み、設問 (1. ー 5.) に答えなさい。

People become vegetarians for many reasons, including the following: health, religious convictions, concerns about animal welfare or the use of antibiotics and hormones in farm animals, or a desire to eat in a way that avoids excessive use of environmental
5 resources. Some people follow a largely vegetarian diet because they can't afford to eat meat. Becoming a vegetarian has become more appealing and accessible, thanks to the all-year availability of fresh produce, more vegetarian options for eating out, and the growing influence of cultures with largely plant-based diets.

10 Approximately six to eight million adults in the United States eat no meat, fish, or poultry, according to a Harris Interactive poll conducted by the Vegetarian Resource Group, a nonprofit organization that spreads information about vegetarianism. Several million more have eliminated red meat but still eat chicken or fish.
15 About two million have become vegans, who are people who avoid not only animal flesh but also animal-based products such as milk, cheese, and eggs.

Traditionally, research into vegetarianism focused mainly on potential nutritional deficiencies, but in recent years, studies are
20 confirming the health benefits of meat-free eating. Nowadays, plant-based eating is recognized as not only nutritionally sufficient but also as a way to reduce the risk for many chronic illnesses. According

to the American Dietetic Association, "appropriately planned vegetarian diets, including total vegetarian or vegan diets, are healthy, nutritionally adequate, and may provide health benefits in the prevention and treatment of certain diseases."

"Appropriately planned" is the key term. Unless you follow recommended guidelines on nutrition, fat consumption, and weight control, becoming a vegetarian won't necessarily be good for you. A diet of soda, cheese pizza, and candy, after all, is technically "vegetarian." For health, it's important to make sure that you eat a wide variety of fruits, vegetables, and whole grains. It's also vital to replace some harmful types of fats with good fats, such as those found in nuts and olive oil. And always keep in mind that if you eat too many calories, even from nutritious, low-fat, plant-based foods, you'll gain weight. So it's also important to practice portion control, read food labels, and engage in regular physical activity.

問 **1.** — **5.** Read the passage and select the best option for questions **1.** - **5.**

1. Which of the following is **NOT** mentioned as a reason for becoming vegetarian?
A. Some people want to be healthier.
B. Some people are too poor to buy meat.
C. Some people want to take antibiotics and hormones efficiently.
D. Some people do not want to be cruel to animals.

2. Which of the following does the poll in the passage report?

A. the number of people who follow various types of vegetarian diets in the U.S.

B. the reasons people become vegetarian

C. statistical information about the health benefits of vegetarian diets

D. what contribution the Vegetarian Resource Group has made to spread vegetarianism

3. What does the third paragraph indicate?

A. People have always believed that vegetarian diets have big potential nutritional benefits.

B. Vegetarian diets can be beneficial as long as they are adequate in nutrition.

C. Vegetarian diets can prevent all illnesses, but they cannot cure some diseases.

D. Vegan diets have been recently recognized as nutritionally insufficient.

4. According to the passage, which of the following statements about "appropriately planned vegetarian diets" is correct?

A. As long as you stick to plant-based eating, you are unlikely to put on weight.

B. Soda, cheese pizza, and candy are meat-free, so they are not bad for health.

C. You should be careful about what kinds of oil and fat you consume.

D. You should only pay attention to nutrition values, not calories, when you choose food.

5. According to the passage, which of the following statements is correct?

A. Vegetarianism has become popular partly because there are more dining-out options for vegetarians now.

B. Cultures with meat-free diets are still minorities, so they have had no impact on the popularity of vegetarianism.

C. Vegans eat meat only when it is fresh, so they are unlikely to become ill.

D. Once you become a vegetarian, you don't have to be concerned about lack of exercise.

制限時間25分／367 words／解答：本冊p.62

次の英文を読み、設問に答えなさい。

1　Understandably, many workers today (1) <u>suffer from</u> job anxiety. They fear losing their jobs to automation and having robots "steal" their (2) <u>livelihoods</u>. It's a legitimate* worry, of course, and not just for blue-collar employees. Many white-collar jobs are (3) <u>vulnerable</u>, too. Let's face it: AI and robots can do many routine jobs more efficiently and more cheaply than human workers. This makes massive layoffs a real possibility. No wonder so many workers are so uneasy.

2　But Martin Feldstein, an economics professor at Harvard, says, "Not to worry." Why? "Simply put: History. For many years, we have been experiencing (4) <u>rapid</u> technological change that substitutes machines and computers for individual workers." But this only means that new, more interesting "human" jobs are being created. (5) <u>At any rate</u>, Feldstein believes that workers have the resilience* it takes to "adjust positively to any changing technology."

3　Business experts don't expect large-scale unemployment to happen either. They (6) <u>predict</u> that most workers won't actually be replaced by robots. Instead, more and more, they will be teamed up with them. What will that be like? How will human workers get along with their machine partners? Dr. Steve Hunt, a business psychologist and systems designer, believes that "digitization" can, paradoxically, create a more human, more (7) <u>productive</u> workplace.

But this can only happen if digitization is applied correctly. Doing that, he says, depends mainly on companies changing their mindset. Most managers, Hunt says, tend to expect workers to perform like machines. They judge employee performance by "tangible*, immediate outcomes that measure the kind of output a machine would produce."

4　This must stop, says Hunt. "We are going to need more and more workers to do the things robots can't do well. Humans excel* at making emotional connections, scanning environments, and (8) recognizing patterns. They can then adapt their behavior to fit the situation." Hunt cites research that shows that human workers almost always treat the robots they work with as living things. Companies must recognize this and incorporate* this information into their management policies. They must prepare for the (9) inevitable social and psychological interactions that will take place between man and machine. Only then, says Hunt, will the "digitized workplace be one that we'll run towards* and not away from."

（注）legitimate* 理にかなった、もっともな　resilience* 柔軟性
　　　tangible* 具体的な、実体のある　　　excel* 優れている
　　　incorporate* 取り入れる　　　　　　towards* toward と同じ

問1　下線部 (1) 〜 (9) の語句の本文中での意味として最も適切なものを、(A) 〜 (D) の中から 1 つ選びなさい。
　(1)　(A)　endure　　　　　(B)　refuse
　　　　(C)　release　　　　　(D)　lack

1 環境
2 社会
3 環境
4 健康
5 IT・テクノロジー
6 医学
7 環境
8 IT・テクノロジー
9 教育
10 社会

(2) (A) sources of pride   (B) sources of knowledge

     (C) sources of love   (D) sources of income

(3) (A) dangerous   (B) at risk

     (C) valuable   (D) troublesome

(4) (A) expected   (B) punctual

     (C) inactive   (D) swift

(5) (A) Anyway   (B) By all means

     (C) For the asking   (D) On average

(6) (A) plan   (B) pretend

     (C) anticipate   (D) regret

(7) (A) dissatisfying   (B) stable

     (C) effective   (D) thoughtful

(8) (A) noticing   (B) ignoring

     (C) considering   (D) recording

(9) (A) preventable   (B) unavoidable

     (C) uncertain   (D) impulsive

問2　(1) ～ (5) の質問の答えとして最も適切なものを、(A) ～ (D) の中から１つ選びなさい。

(1)　According to paragraph 1, which of the following is true?

    (A)　It's unreasonable to be afraid of robots.

    (B)　People don't want to do routine jobs anymore.

    (C)　Blue-collar workers don't worry much about robots.

    (D)　A lot of people might lose their jobs in the future.

(2)　According to paragraph 2, which of the following is true?

    (A)　Technological change creates new employment opportunities.

    (B)　Human workers can't handle the changes that are taking place.

    (C)　Good jobs will soon be history.

    (D)　In the past, technology has seldom eliminated jobs.

(3) According to paragraph 3, which of the following is true?
- (A) Human employees and robots will be divided into separate groups.
- (B) Humans will become "digitized" in order to compete with robots.
- (C) These days, many companies want human employees to work in a robotic way.
- (D) Companies have to control how their employees think.

(4) According to paragraph 4, which of the following is true?
- (A) Humans are better than robots at understanding the feelings of others.
- (B) Workplaces with many robots will require them to scan the environment.
- (C) The minds of robots are often too difficult to understand for humans.
- (D) Robots can adapt to situations well because they are not alive.

(5) Which of the following is the best title for the passage?
- (A) The History of Robots in the Workplace
- (B) The Future of Work
- (C) Robots: The Best Workers
- (D) Work Like a Machine

次の英文を読んで、後の問いに答えよ。

In many parts of the world, children are told to drink milk every day because doing so will give them strong bones. The idea does make some sense. Milk contains calcium, and calcium is known to improve bone density.

5　　But (1) demonstrating a definite link between milk consumption and bone density is more complex than it sounds. The ideal study would take two large groups of people and assign every member of one group to drink plenty of milk daily for several decades, while the other group would drink some kind of milk substitute instead.

10　(2), this is too difficult to do (3) in practice.

What we can do instead is to take thousands of people, ask them how much milk they've been drinking over the years, and then follow them for at least a decade to see whether those who regularly drink milk are any less likely to suffer from broken bones later in life.

15　This is what happened in an article published in 1997 by Harvard University researchers. An impressive 77,000 female nurses were followed for 10 years. In that study, researchers found no significant difference in the numbers of broken arms or hips between people who drank one glass of milk a week or less and those who drank two

20　or more.

To confuse things further, in 2014 came the results of two large Swedish studies which led to headlines that drinking more than three glasses of milk a day — a larger amount than most people drink — was no help to your bones, and might even harm you.

25 　But before we (4) <u>pour away</u> the milk, there are some important things to take into account. For example, in the Swedish studies, the people who took part were required to estimate their milk consumption during the previous years, which is no easy task. It's hard to know how much you eat with cereal, or in tea, or in cooking. 30 So, until we know more, the current weight of evidence suggests that it is still OK to continue to drink milk if you like it. It probably does have benefits for bone health, even though such benefits are shorter-lived than you might have hoped.

注　bone density　骨密度　　　consumption (noun) > consume (verb)

1.　下線部 (1)、(3)、(4) に代わる語句として最も適切なものを選択肢から選び、その記号をマークせよ。

(1)　demonstrating
　　　A. examining　　　　　B. finding
　　　C. protesting　　　　　D. showing

(3)　in practice
　　　A. in training　　　　　B. in reality
　　　C. without effort　　　　D. without preparation

(4)　pour away
　　　A. dispose of　　　　　B. finish
　　　C. reduce　　　　　　　D. throw up

2. 空所（　2　）に入る最も適切なものを選択肢から選び、その記号をマークせよ。

A. In addition
B. Fortunately
C. Obviously
D. Therefore

3. 第3、4パラグラフの内容と一致するものを選択肢から1つ選び、その記号をマークせよ。

A. An alternative way to investigate how milk consumption is related to bone density is to survey thousands of people after tracking their health for at least ten years.

B. The question concerns a possible correlation between ageing and bone density among regular milk-drinkers.

C. In the Harvard University study that appeared in 1997, researchers were greatly impressed by the health of more than 70,000 female nurses.

D. In the Harvard study, the quantity of milk consumed by individuals did not have a significant impact on the frequency of broken arms or hips.

4. 第5、6パラグラフの内容と一致するものを選択肢から2つ選び、その記号をマークせよ。

A. Two later studies in 2014 were reported as suggesting that above-average consumption of milk might have negative consequences for physical health.

B. What we decide to do about milk should wait until we calculate exactly how much we regularly consume.

C. It is not obvious how to guess how much milk one consumes on a daily or yearly basis.

D. In the absence of definite proof, an appreciation of milk adds to the evidence in support of drinking it.

E. Although drinking milk is probably good for your bones, you might live longer than you could.

次の英文を読み、後の問いに答えよ。

The world's population is expected to grow from around 7.3 billion today to more than 9 billion by 2050, and is quite likely to reach 11 billion by the end of the 21st century. Will the world's farms and fisheries be able to feed all those people? Probably not. Already, approximately 800 million people in the world cannot get enough to eat. While the main cause of hunger now is poverty, in the future, the biggest factor may be food shortages, due to unsustainable farming practices, the impacts of global warming, and the relentless* increase in the world's population.

Climate change is already damaging agriculture in many countries, with longer and more frequent droughts in some areas and flooding in others, and the situation is bound to get worse. However, agriculture is not just a victim of climate change, it is also a major cause, responsible for significant greenhouse gas emissions and for the clearing of forests to create more farmland.

In order to feed more people later this century and to reduce the impact of agriculture on our climate, we will need to use our limited farmland much more efficiently. One use of agricultural land that is particularly wasteful is for raising cattle or growing cattle feed. To produce 1 kilogram of beef from grain-fed cattle, at least 7 kilograms of grain are needed. If we all gave up eating beef, a lot more people could be fed. Another wasteful use of farmland is to produce corn, palm oil, and other crops for use as bio-ethanol in car engines. <u>Feeding cars instead of people is not only wasteful but also very unethical.</u>

FAO** research has shown that about one third of all food produced worldwide is eventually wasted. There are various reasons for this, such as inadequate storage and transportation facilities in developing countries, the rejection by retailers or consumers of fruits and vegetables whose color, size or shape is below standard, and the removal of food from stores when it passes its expiry date.

The amount of food thrown away in Japan could feed more than 30 million people each year. Japan is a significant consumer of meat, mainly beef, pork, and chicken. Japanese consumers could make a contribution to the looming*** food crisis and to reducing their impact on the world's climate by wasting less food and eating less meat.

*relentless「絶え間のない」
**FAO Food and Agriculture Organization「国連食糧農業機関」
*** looming「迫り来る」

問1 本文の第１段落の内容に合うものとして最も適当なものを、ア～エから１つ選びなさい。

ア．Farmers and fishermen will demonstrate their ability to produce enough food for the world in the coming years.

イ．In days to come, the increase in the temperature of the earth may become one of the factors leading to starvation in the world.

ウ．It is assumed that the world's population will drop by about 1.7 billion by the mid-21st century.

エ．There are no more than 700 million people who cannot get enough food to eat.

問2 本文の第２段落の内容に<u>合わないもの</u>を、ア～エから１つ選びなさい。

ア．Even though there are unusually large amounts of rain, agriculture will not be affected in the future.

イ．Farming is largely affected by weather events such as droughts and flooding.

ウ．The expansion of land for agriculture also involves cutting down trees and thus contributes to changes in the climate.

エ．The negative influence of climate change will also surely be damaging to agriculture.

問3 下線部の内容に合うものとして最も適当なものを、ア～エから１つ選びなさい。

ア．Automobiles that use fuel obtained from crops such as corn is an efficient use of resources.

イ．Considering the limited amount of farmland, we should use it to produce food rather than fuel.

ウ．Corn should be used for fueling cars rather than grown to produce beef for human consumption.

エ．It is neither wasteful nor unethical to feed cars instead of people.

問4 本文の第3段落の内容に合うものとして最も適当なものを、ア～エから1つ選びなさい。

ア．Because so much farmland is used for the raising of animals for human consumption, our farmland is being wasted.

イ．Producing palm oil is an efficient use of farmland when it is used to power cars.

ウ．We need more effective management of our farmland, such as increasing the amount used to produce food for cattle.

エ．We need not be concerned about how we use farmland because there is more than enough of it.

問5 本文の第4段落の内容に<u>合わないもの</u>を、ア～エから1つ選びなさい。

ア．According to FAO, a certain quantity of food produced in the world is thrown away.

イ．Food not being stored and delivered as it should be in developing countries can lead to waste.

ウ．One reason for sellers or customers not to accept fruit is because of its poor quality.

エ．Waste does not result from shopkeepers throwing out food from their stores that has passed its date of expiry.

問6 本文の第5段落の内容に合うものとして最も適当なものを、ア～エから1つ選びなさい。

ア．Even if the Japanese reduce their animal product consumption, this would not have any impact on the food crisis.

イ．It can be said that meat hardly makes up an important part of Japanese diets.

ウ．Japanese customers could make a more useful contribution by eating larger quantities of meat.

エ．Japanese people are big eaters of meat and they also dispose of large amounts of uneaten food.

ア．The writer doubts that nowadays the state of being poor is the most significant cause of hunger.

イ．Some of the blame for the world's climate change is due to agricultural practices.

ウ．In the process of climate change, the growing of crops only functions as a cause of greenhouse gasses.

エ．It is possible that if people refrain from eating beef, there will be more food for people in the world.

オ．From an ethical point of view, supplying food for people should come first before its use as fuel for automobiles.

カ．Over 30 million additional people could be fed if Japanese people did not throw away food.

キ．People in Japan may reduce the effect they have on the climate with less food waste and less meat consumption.

制限時間25分／**474 words**／解答：本冊**p.98**

次の文章を読み、問い（A 〜 E）に答えなさい。なお、＊のついた語は注がある。

People have long imagined a world where we interact with computers and robots as if they were normal human beings. Science fiction movies such as Her and Chappie show computers and robots that think and feel just like humans. While scenarios like these exist only in the movies for now, we may be getting close to making technology emotionally intelligent.

The first step toward this is understanding what （　ア　）are. It's a complicated area of study. Scientists are often unable to define emotions in exact terms, even though we generally understand what people mean when they say they're sad or happy.

Back in the 1950s, few scientists studied emotion. But American psychologist Paul Ekman saw a lot of potential in this field. He began analyzing facial expressions, and compiled a list of over 5,000 muscle movements. These muscle movements combine to form our different expressions. His discovery of micro expressions — facial expressions that last only a fraction of a second — allows us to read the emotions that people try to hide. A number of technology companies have now started to use Dr. Ekman's work to create software that recognizes human facial expressions. By analyzing thousands of different faces, the software learns to recognize different emotions with greater and greater accuracy.

There are many possible uses of emotion-sensing technology. Dr. Chieko Asakawa, a researcher at Carnegie Mellon University, has been blind since the age of 14. She has been developing a smartphone app that might be able to help people with disabilities. Using the smartphone's camera and audio, the app helps the user navigate their environment. It also recognizes people's faces and facial expressions as they approach. Dr. Asakawa is working to refine the (1) {①app ②enable ③it ④moods ⑤people's ⑥to read ⑦to}.

Another use of emotion-sensing technology can be illustrated through human-shaped robots like Pepper. *Launched in Japan in 2015, Pepper is an interactive companion robot. It's capable of recognizing basic human emotions and responding appropriately. For example, it comforts someone when (2)it senses the person is sad, or cracks a joke when the person is feeling playful. In Japan, Pepper is already serving customers in retail stores.

Although the idea of emotionally intelligent devices may sound fascinating, this technology can create some major challenges. The issue of privacy is something that many people, including Paul Ekman, are concerned about. (イ), as we walk on the streets, devices and scanners could record our facial expressions without our knowledge. This could allow many people to monitor or view our feelings without permission. It may leave us no control over who we share our feelings with. However, if we can negotiate these challenges successfully, there could be many benefits for all of us if our devices become a little more human.

(注) launch「…を発売する」

A 文中の（　ア　）、（　イ　）に入れるのに最も適当な語句を、次の①
　　～④から１つずつ選び、番号で答えなさい。
（　ア　）
　① scientists　　　　② emotions
　③ scenarios　　　　④ computers

（　イ　）
　① For example　　　② Therefore
　③ However　　　　　④ In addition

B Paul Ekmanについて本文の記述に最も合うものを、次の①～④
　　の中から１つ選び、番号で答えなさい。
　① Paul Ekman was one of the few scientists who studied
　　emotion in the 1980s.
　② Paul Ekman thought there were a lot of things to learn
　　from the study of emotion.
　③ Paul Ekman didn't recognize that muscles on the face
　　move a little when we try to hide our emotions.
　④ Paul Ekman thought we should stop using technology,
　　which does harm to the environment.

C (1)の{　　}内の語句を意味が通るように並べ替えたとき、４番
　　目にくる語句は①～⑦のうちどれか。番号で答えなさい。

D 下線部(2)のitの指示内容として最も適当なものを、次の①～④の
　　中から１つ選び、番号で答えなさい。
　① human　　　　　② emotion
　③ Pepper　　　　　④ technology

本文の内容と合っているものを、次の①〜⑧から３つ選び、番号で
答えなさい。ただし、答えの順序は問わない。

① In the movies, Her and Chappie, humans acted and felt
   like robots.

② With further study of emotion, we may be able to make
   technology emotionally intelligent.

③ Technology companies are now trying to create software
   that can recognize different emotions accurately.

④ Dr. Chieko Asakawa has been developing a smartphone
   app which makes use of emotion-sensing technology.

⑤ Pepper was invented by Dr. Chieko Asakawa to help
   people navigate the environment around them.

⑥ In Japan, Pepper, which was launched in 2015, can now
   serve food to customers.

⑦ Emotion-sensing technology hasn't created any problems
   that we need to worry about.

⑧ One of the benefits of emotion-sensing technology is that
   many people can record our facial expressions without
   our knowledge.

1 環境
2 社会
3 環境
4 健康
5 ＩＴ・テクノロジー
6 医学
7 環境
8 ＩＴ・テクノロジー
9 教育
10 社会

制限時間20分／492 words／解答：本冊p.110

次の英文を読み、設問に答えなさい。

Although many people think it is a modern phenomenon, distance learning has been around for at least 200 years in one form or another. Historical examples of long-distance learning include students being sent a series of weekly lessons by mail. The technological advances of the past 20 or so years, however, have meant that this form of education is now a credible alternative to face-to-face learning. (1)Indeed, 1996 saw the establishment of the world's first "virtual university" in the United States, showing how far distance learning has come in a relatively short space of time. While it is now possible to obtain a large variety of online degrees, which is the best type of education to pursue? A closer examination of this topic reveals that distance and traditional educational instruction have significant differences but also some similarities.

When comparing the two systems, the most obvious difference lies in the way that instruction is delivered. Distance learning is heavily dependent on technology, particularly the Internet. In a face-to-face course, students may only require a computer for the purpose of writing an essay. In comparison, when learning remotely, technology is the principal means of communication. Face-to-face instruction must take place in real time and in one location. Conversely, distance learning can happen at any time and in any location, since the learning is not restricted by geography. (2)The flexibility this provides means that students may be better able to learn at their own pace, but it may also mean that learners have to be well organized and self-disciplined. In other words, they must be more highly motivated in order to do well in distance-learning courses. Finally, with face-to-face learning, the teacher and student have the opportunity to develop a personal relationship. In a virtual classroom, by contrast, the teacher may seldom or never actually meet the student. (3)This may make it hard for teachers to understand their students' specific learning needs.

Although the nature of the teacher-student relationship may differ in the two methods, they do share the same (A)core principles. Just as a teacher is the "knower" in a classroom, he or she is the one responsible for helping students understand the key sections of an online course. The teacher needs to decide how to best present the material to be learned and in which sequence the topics should be introduced. He or she must also create the assignments for the course and help the students know what resources (textbooks, websites, and so on) will best support their learning. Additionally, a teacher needs to provide student feedback in some way. For example, a language teacher in a classroom may be able to correct a student's grammar or pronunciation in the moment, whereas a distance-learning teacher may need to provide written or recorded feedback to be delivered later. In any case, all the usual elements of the teacher's role are necessary, no matter what kind of instruction is being used.

設問1 下線部 (1) を日本語に訳しなさい。

設問2 下線部 (2) を、this の内容も明らかにして、日本語に訳しなさい。

設問3 下線部 (3) を、This の内容も明らかにして、日本語に訳しなさい。

設問4 下線部 (A) について、本文に基づいて日本語で説明しなさい。

次の英文を読んで、後の問い（ 問1 ～ 問5 ）に答えなさい。

① Recently, alternative work styles are giving workers the opportunity to work in totally different environments. Imagine making a cup of coffee in your kitchen and starting to work by turning on your computer in your office at home. This recent trend is called "telecommuting" or "teleworking." Some companies have closed their offices and all of their employees and managers are telecommuting. Other companies have assigned certain employees to work in this way. Telecommuting eliminates the rush hour commute for workers and saves companies thousands of dollars in rent and utilities for office space. Will more companies consider working at home or other alternative work styles? Does this mean that the traditional work style will fade away in the future? A number of companies are using a combination of traditional and alternative work styles. Many workers and companies are looking for more flexibility to help make their work and personal lives more convenient, efficient and productive. Some companies claim that alternative work styles lead to higher productivity. These new working styles are already being practiced in many technology companies.

② Alternative work styles are increasing in popularity because the technology supports a more mobile working style. However, workers spend about 40 years of their lives in jobs, so the work environment is an important concern. This trend has created other alternative working styles including "open seating" or "hotdesking," "officing," "hoteling," and "co-working." "Open seating" or "hotdesking" is a system where workers do not have assigned desks. They come into the office and sit at a group of desks on a first-come, first-served basis. Another similar concept is mobile desks or "officing." Mobile desks can be moved into different arrangements for individual work or teamwork. These also have proven to be efficient for workers and financially rewarding for companies.

③ <u>Moreover</u>, alternative work styles can also include relocating to other work spaces. "Hoteling" can be used for consultants or other freelance groups that only need office space for a short period. Seating at desks in the office is arranged by the company only when needed. "Co-working" is a very different alternative work style. Co-working spaces in apartment buildings combine the informal atmosphere of the home office with a relaxed coffee lounge environment. Co-workers rent a private desk in the apartment and share the common areas, which may include meeting areas, office equipment and lounge space. "Co-working" can help solve feelings of isolation and loneliness for some telecommuters.

④ <u>On</u> the other hand, working at home or in other alternative work styles is not always the perfect solution. Some workers may try too hard to meet their employer's expectations. This could result in increased stress and overwork. Meeting new business contacts is more limited, and some workers feel more isolated. The traditional

1 環境
2 社会
3 環境
4 健康
5 IT・テクノロジー
6 医学
7 環境
8 IT・テクノロジー
9 教育
10 社会

office is not only a business environment but also an important social environment. Some workers feel more comfortable socially in a traditional office. Hopefully, more research will help to identify the challenges of alternative work styles that companies and workers will have to cope with in the future.

問1 下線部①Recentlyで始まる段落の内容と一致するものを1つ選びなさい。

① Alternative life styles cannot be practiced while telecommuting.

② Telecommuting allows workers to communicate through the internet with their families.

③ Telecommuting permits flexible working hours and encourages office interaction.

④ Avoiding busy traffic times is one benefit for telecommuting employees.

問2 下線部②Alternativeで始まる段落の内容と一致しないものを1つ選びなさい。

① Technology helps workers be more flexible about where they can work.

② The work space atmosphere is important for those employed there for decades.

③ Not having assigned desks has proven productive.

④ Hotdesking and officing enable employees to work from home.

問3 下線部③Moreover で始まる段落の内容と一致するものを 1 つ選び
なさい。

① 共有スペースで仕事をすることは、その利用者の孤独感の軽減
につながる。

② 一時的にホテルの部屋で仕事をすることは、経費節約型のオル
タナティブワークである。

③ カフェを仕事場として利用することは、オルタナティブワーク
の特徴である。

④ ホテルの部屋を仕事場として利用する場合、利用者が部屋の予
約をする必要がない。

問4 下線部④On で始まる段落の内容と一致するものを 1 つ選びなさ
い。

① Alternative work styles create more stress on bosses.

② Technology in traditional offices makes employees
comfortable.

③ Social and business communication in an office is not
replaced easily.

④ Those who experience increased tension and loneliness
can work at home.

問5 本文の内容と一致するものを 1 つ選びなさい。

① Sharing work spaces and changing office seating
arrangements can be effective.

② Shared lounges are vital to the success of hotdesking
and hoteling.

③ Traditional offices do not function as social
environments.

④ The problems of employee isolation and stress may be
solved by telecommuting.

大学入試

レベル別
英語長文問題
Solution
ソリューション

最新テーマ編

1/
スタンダード
レベル

スタディサプリ
英語講師
肘井 学
Gaku Hijii

かんき出版

　"新時代の英語長文集を作ること"。このテーマで『大学入試レベル別英語長文問題ソリューション1～3』を執筆させていただきました。「解いて終わり」の英語長文はもう終わりにして、「出てきた単語を必ず覚える、そして音読を10回することで、1文1文を自分のものにして先に進む」というコンセプトは、たくさんの賛同をいただき、多くの教育者の方々に推奨していただけるほどになりました。

　本書は、前作の「音読がしやすい語数」という最大の特長を維持しつつ、その語数を音読可能な500語台にまで広げて、最新のテーマを扱うという趣旨の英語長文問題集です。食品廃棄問題、AI、自動運転車、海洋汚染、菜食主義、プラスチックごみ、遠隔教育など、最新のトレンドを扱っています。これらの分野から本番の試験問題が出題される可能性は非常に高いと言っても差し支えないでしょう。

　もっとも、入試本番で、本書で扱ったものと同じテーマや同じ文章が出ても、決して油断しないようにしてください。知っている題材や読み込んだ文章が試験に出題されることは大きなアドバンテージになりますが、あくまで試験当日に見た文章から、客観的に情報を読み取り、その情報から答えを推論すること、これだけは忘れないでください。

　長文中に出てきた単語を必ず覚えること、そして音読を10回することは、魔法のような相乗効果をもたらしてくれます。さあ、さっそく本書で音読のパワーを最大限に味わってください！　皆さんが信じるべきは、毎日の己の地道な努力であることを、お忘れないように。

肘井　学

目　　次

背景知識が
広がるコラム

BACKGROUND KNOWLEDGE

本シリーズの特長

特長その❶　4種類のポイントで万全の英語力が身に付く!

　本書では、一文一文の理解に役立つ 構文 POINT 、文と文のつながりを見抜く 論理 POINT 、問題の解き方がわかる 解法 POINT 、語彙の本質に強くなる 語彙 POINT と、4種類の **POINT** で体系化してあらゆる角度から英語力を向上させていきます（p.8〜p.9参照）。

特長その❷　文構造がひと目でわかる構文図解付き!

　構文図解で、SVOCMの記号を使って、解釈の手助けをします。必要に応じて、▲マークで**細かい文法事項のメモを入れており**、**独学でも疑問を残しません**。これと全訳を照らし合わせて、問題を解き終わった後に、**一文一文丁寧に構文把握**をします。

特長その❸　音読用白文・リスニング強化の音声ダウンロード付き!

　音読用の白文を掲載しています。**音声ダウンロード**を利用して、音声の後に英文の音読を続けて、**リスニング強化・正確な発音習得**にも役立ててください。問題を解く ⇒ 解説を読む ⇒ 構文把握する ⇒ 単語を覚えた後の**音読10回を必ず行ってください**。

特長その❹　単語帳代わりになる語彙リスト付き!

　本書では、本文訳の下に**語彙リスト**を掲載しています。必ず、**出てきた単語をその場で覚えて**ください。

特長その❺　背景知識が広がるコラム付き!

　すべての英文に、背景知識が広がるコラムを設けました。背景知識としてあると、**英文を読むのが非常に楽になる**ものを、コラムで紹介しています。自由英作文にはもちろん、他科目にも有効な一生モノの知識が詰まっています。

時代を反映した最新の頻出テーマである「**食品廃棄問題**」・「**人工知能**」・「**海洋汚染**」・「**菜食主義**」・「**プラスチックごみ問題**」・「**働き方改革**」など、長文の題材を厳選しました。将来の教養として、興味深い題材がそろっています。

志望大学に左右されない確かな英語力を養うために、出典を**国公立大学と私立大学からバランスよく**選びました。スタンダードレベルなので、出典は私立大学が中心ですが、国公立大学もしっかり扱っています。同時に、**文系と理系の両方に精通できる**ような内容を、バランスよく配置しています。

どの形式でも対応できる英語力を付けるために、**マーク式と記述式の問題をバランスよく配置**しました。さらに、実際の入試問題から、**悪問や奇問を外して、良問をそろえました。**

本書で推奨する**音読10回**をやり遂げるために、**音読が可能な300語〜500語前後の英文をそろえました。**前作で好評を博した300語前後の文章に加えて、500語前後の文章も扱うことで、より幅広いテーマの英文を扱うことを可能にしました。

4 種 類 の POINT

構文 POINT

論理 POINT

本シリーズの使い方

❶　問題を解く

　各問題には、制限時間を設けています。それを参考に、**1題20分〜 30分程度**で、本番を想定して問題を解きます。

↓

❷　解答・解説を見て答え合わせをする

　悪問・奇問の類は外しています。**4種類のポイント**を中心に解説を読み進めてください。**解答の根拠となる部分は太字で示しています。**

↓

❸　英文全体の構文把握や意味を理解する

　構文図解と全訳を参考にして、全文を理解します。**主語と動詞の把握**、修飾語のカタマリと役割を把握して、**全文の構文**を確認していきます。

↓

❹　知らない単語を必ず覚える

　語彙リストを利用して、**英語・日本語セットで3回書いて、10回唱えて**ください。単語学習のコツは、何度も繰り返すことです。

↓

❺　音声を聞きながら、後に続けて音読を10回する

　音声を右ページを参考にダウンロードして、**音声に合わせて、テキストを見ながら10回音読**をします。句や節といった意味の切れ目を意識して音読してください。10回目に近付くにつれて、**英語を英語のまま理解できる**いわゆる英語脳に近付くことができます。③と④の工程をしっかりやることが、**スムーズに音読できる最大のコツ**であることを覚えておいてください。

本シリーズのレベル設定

　本シリーズは、現状の学力に見合った学習を促すために、下記の表のように、細かいレベル分けをしています。

スタンダード レベル	日本大、東洋大、駒沢大、専修大や、京都産業大、近畿大、甲南大、龍谷大などに代表される私立大学を目指す人、共通テストでの平均点以上や地方国公立大を目指す人。
ハイレベル	学習院大、明治大、青山学院大、立教大、中央大、法政大や、関西大、関西学院大、同志社大、立命館大などの難関私大を目指す人。共通テストでの高得点や上位公立大を目指す人。
トップレベル	早稲田大、慶応大、上智大、東京理科大などの最難関私大を目指す。共通テストで満点や、北大、東北大、東京大、名古屋大、京都大、大阪大、九州大などの難関国公立大を目指す人。

難易度のレベルには変動があり、あくまでも目安です。

音声ダウンロードの方法

 ヘッドフォンマークの中の番号は音声ファイル内のトラック番号です。

パソコンかスマートフォンで、
右のQRコードを読み取るか

https://kanki-pub.co.jp/pages/ghsaishins/

にアクセスして、音声ファイルをダウンロードしてください。

※音声ダウンロードについてのお問合せ先：https://kanki-pub.co.jp/pages/infodl/

● 句と節について

　句と節とは、両方とも**意味のカタマリ**と思っていただいて大丈夫です。例えば、When he woke up, the class was over. では、When he woke up までが1つの意味のカタマリで、そこに he woke up という**SV の文構造があると、節**といいます。かつ When he woke up は was を修飾する副詞の働きをしているので、**副詞節**といいます。

　また、I like to read comics. という文では、to read comics が「漫画を読むこと」という意味のカタマリを作っており、そこに**SV がないので、句**といいます。かつ to read comics は「漫画を読むこと」という名詞のカタマリなので、**名詞句**といいます。

　節は、**名詞節・形容詞節・副詞節**、句は**名詞句・形容詞句・副詞句**と、意味のカタマリを分類すると、6種類があります。

● カッコについて

　名詞のカタマリ（名詞句・名詞節）は〈　　　〉で表します。**形容詞のカタマリ（形容詞句・形容詞節）は（　　　）で表し、前の名詞を修飾します。副詞のカタマリ（副詞句・副詞節）は[　　　]で表し、動詞を修飾します。**

● 文の要素について

　英文の各パーツを理解するために、**S（主語）、V（動詞）、O（目的語）、C（補語）、M（修飾語）**という5つの要素に振り分けます。無理にこの5つに当てはめないほうがいい場合は、何も記号を振りません。

　Sは、I go to school. の I のような**日本語の「〜は・が」に当たる部分**です。**V**は、go のような**日本語の「〜する」に当たる部分**です。**O**は I like soccer. の soccer のような**動詞の目的語**です。**C**は、I am a teacher. の a teacher のように、**主語やときに目的語の補足説明**をする部分です。

● 品詞について

　名詞・形容詞・副詞・前置詞が役割をおさえるべき主要な品詞です。**名詞**は、I like soccer.のように、Iという名詞が**文のS**になったり、soccerという名詞が**文のO**になったり、I am a teacher.のa teacherのように**C**になります。**名詞は文のS・O・Cのいずれかになります。**

　形容詞は、a cute girlのcuteのように**名詞を修飾**するか、He is old.のoldのように**補語**になります。**形容詞は、名詞を修飾するか文の補語になるかのいずれかです。**

　副詞は、very goodのveryのように、うしろの**副詞や形容詞を修飾**します。You can see the world clearly.のclearlyのように「はっきりと見える」と**動詞を修飾**したり、Clearly, you need to exercise.のClearlyのように「明らかに、あなたは運動する必要がある」と、**文を修飾**したりします。**副詞は名詞以外の形容詞・副詞・動詞・文を修飾します。**

　前置詞は、The train for Osaka will arrive at nine.のforのように、for Osaka「大阪行きの」という**形容詞のカタマリを作って前の名詞The trainを修飾**したり、atのようにat nine「9時に」という**副詞のカタマリを作って動詞arriveを修飾**したりします。**前置詞は形容詞のカタマリと副詞のカタマリを作ります。**

● 具体と抽象について

　抽象とは、簡単に言うと、**まとめ・まとまり**のことです。それを**具体例**を用いて、わかりやすく説明していくのが、英語に最もよく見られる論理展開です。例えば、

「彼は、**複数の言語**を話すことができる」

「例えば、**日本語・英語・中国語**など」

　上の例では、「**（彼の話すことのできる）複数の言語**」が抽象表現に当たり、「**日本語・英語・中国語**」が具体例です。このつながりが見えてくると、英語長文の理解がグンと深まります。

● 因果関係について

　因果関係とは、原因と結果の関係のことです。英語の世界では、**こういった原因から、この結果が生まれたという因果関係をとても重視**します。例えば、「昨日とても夜遅くに寝た」という原因から、「今日はとても眠い」という結果が生まれます。

● パラフレーズについて

　本書では、**パラフレーズ（言い換え）**という用語を多用しています。本来はphrase「句」という一定の意味のカタマリの言い換えに使いますが、本書では**単語の言い換え、文の言い換えにまで幅広くパラフレーズという用語を使っている**ので、ご承知おきください。

● 関係詞について

　関係代名詞（which, who, that, what）と**関係副詞**（when, where, why, how）があります。基本は、**形容詞のカタマリを作って前の名詞を説明する働き**です。例えば、

This is the book **which** I like the best.

「これは私がいちばん好きな本です」

のように、the book に which 以下が説明を加えます。

● 不定詞について

　to ＋ 動詞の原形 **を不定詞**といいます。Ｓ・Ｏ・Ｃで使う**名詞的用法**「〜すること」、名詞を修飾する**形容詞的用法**「〜する（ための）」、動詞を修飾する**副詞的用法**「〜するために」があります。例えば、

I want something hot **to drink**.「温かい飲み物がほしい」

の**to drink** が**不定詞の形容詞的用法**で、something hot「温かいもの」を修飾しています。

● 分詞と分詞構文について

　分詞には、**現在分詞**（doing）と**過去分詞**（done）があります。**形容詞として使用**すると、the window **broken** by the boy「その少年が割った窓」のように、**名詞の後ろにおいて説明を加えます**。

　一方で、**分詞を副詞として使用**すると、**分詞構文**になります。全部で3パターンあり、① Doing（Done）〜 , SV.、② S, doing（done）〜 , V.、③ SV 〜 , doing（done）.... です。例えば、

Seeing his parents, he ran away.

「両親を見ると、彼は逃げ去った」

のSeeing 〜 が分詞構文で、「〜すると」と接続詞の意味を補って訳します。

1

太陽光エネルギー

別冊p.2／制限時間20分／381 words

解答

問1 ②　　問2 ①　　問3 ③　　問4 ③　　問5 ②

解説

問1

この文章によると、太陽熱発電は [　　　]。
① 太陽光をとらえるために使用される
② 太陽光で物を熱することだ
③ 「太陽から生まれること」を意味する
④ ガラスやプラスチックのように太陽光をとらえる

solar thermal power「太陽熱発電」は、第2段落第1文 'Solar' means 'coming from the sun', so when you use sunlight to make things hot, it is called solar thermal power. 「『ソーラー』とは『太陽から生まれること』を意味するので、物を熱くするのに太陽光を使うと、太陽熱発電と呼ばれる」の中に登場する。この文から、②が正解。③はあくまでsolarの説明なので不適。①、④は本文に記述なし。

問2

太陽熱発電の例として挙げられていないものはどれか。
① ソーラーライト　　② 太陽熱調理器
③ 太陽熱温水器　　　④ 建物の暖房

第2段落第3文 In Africa, people use solar cookers.「アフリカでは、人は太陽熱調理器を使う」の文に着目する。

論理 POINT ❶ 固有名詞は具体例の目印

　抽象と具体のつながりがわかると、文章の理解がぐんと深まります。**固有名詞は具体例の目印**になるので、何の具体例なのかを考えます。

　第2段落第3文の **In Africa**、第6文の **Turkey and China** という固有名詞に**着目**する。すると、**solar thermal power を使っている地域の具体例**を表すとわかるので、第3文、第6文の前に「**例えば**」を補って、文のつながりを見抜いていく。太陽熱発電の具体例として、「例えばアフリカでは太陽熱調理器を使い、例えばトルコや中国では、屋根に太陽熱温水器を取り付ける」とわかる。したがって、②、③も太陽熱発電の具体例なので、不適。

　第2段落第2文 **Many buildings use materials like glass and plastic to catch sunlight and warm the building.**「**多くの建物が、太陽光をとらえて建物を暖かくするために、ガラスやプラスチックのような資材を使う**」は、前文の solar thermal power の具体例の1つで、太陽熱発電の例として挙げられているので、④も不適。①の solar lights は第4段落に登場するが、**太陽電池を使った具体的な商品で、太陽熱発電とは異なる**ので、これが正解になる。

問3

　この文章によると、太陽電池について何が正しいか。
　①　それらは、当たる太陽光のほとんどを利用する。
　②　それらは高価ではない。
　③　それらは、粒子の動きによって電気を作り出す。
　④　それらは、お湯を沸かすのに使われる。

　第3段落第2文 **When sunlight hits the silicon, particles inside it move, and this makes electricity.**「**太陽光がそのシリコンに当たると、その中の粒子が動いて、電気が発生する**」の the silicon は太陽電池の素材なので、③が正解。

　不正解の選択肢を見ていくと、①、②は、**第4段落第1文 At the moment, the best solar cells can only use about 25 percent of the sunlight that hits them, and they are an expensive way to** produce electricity.「今のところ、最高の太陽電池でも、それを照らす太陽光のおよそ25%しか使用できないので、太陽電池は、電気を生み出すにはお金がかかる方法だ」に反するので不適。④は第2段落のsolar thermal powerの具体例なので不適。

- -

問4

この文章によると、現在どんな移動手段が太陽熱発電を利用しているか。

① 車、列車、ボート   ② 列車、バス、飛行機

③ 飛行機、車、ボート   ④ ボート、車、バス

最終段落第1文より、同段落の内容が、太陽熱発電が移動手段に使われる説明とわかる。同段落第2文より飛行機、第5文よりソーラーボート、第6文で車が登場するので、③が正解。第5文は、あくまで現時点ではソーラーボートがあるだけで、ソーラーバスやソーラートレインは将来登場する可能性があると言っているだけであることに注意する。

- -

問5

この文章を最もよく要約したものはどれか。

① 人はもっと太陽光発電を利用すべきだ。

② 太陽光発電はたくさん応用されている。

③ 太陽光発電はより安くなりつつある。

④ ソーラー航空機は、驚くべきものだ。

②は、第2段落のsolar thermal power、第3段落のsolar cells、第5段落の移動手段にも太陽光発電が使われていることから、正解。①は**should use「利用すべき」**が本文に記述なし。③は**第4段落第2文 cheaper solar cells「より安価な太陽電池」**と、本文中に話題として出てくるが、**要約ではないので不適**。④はamazing「驚くべきものだ」が本文に記述なし。

A Bright Future

The sunlight (that reaches Earth in one hour) has as much energy
[as all the power that people use in a year]. But how can we get
this energy and use it [on earth]?

'Solar' means ⟨'coming from the sun'⟩, so [when you use sunlight
to make things hot], it is called solar thermal power. Many buildings
use materials (like glass and plastic) [to catch sunlight and warm
the building]. [In Africa], people use solar cookers. [When light hits
the surface of the cooker], it is reflected [into the middle]. The
middle becomes hot [enough to heat water or cook food]. [In
countries like Turkey and China], people put solar water heaters [on
their roofs]. These are metal and glass boxes (with water pipes in
them). The glass catches heat and the metal reflects sunlight [onto
the water pipes], which carry the hot water down [into the houses].

We can use sunlight [to make electricity] too, [with devices called
solar cells], which are made of silicon. [When sunlight hits the
silicon], particles (inside it) move, and this makes electricity. One
solar cell does not produce much power, so we put the cells together
[to make big solar panels].

明るい未来

　1時間の間に地球に届く太陽光は、人間が1年で使うすべての電力と同じくらいのエネルギーを持つ。しかし、私たちは地球で、どうやってこのエネルギーを得て使うことができているのだろうか。

　「ソーラー」とは「太陽から生まれること」を意味するので、物を熱くするのに太陽光を使うと、それは太陽熱発電と呼ばれる。多くの建物が、太陽光をとらえて建物を暖かくするために、ガラスやプラスチックのような資材を使っている。アフリカでは、太陽熱調理器を使う。太陽光が調理器の表面に当たると、中心部に反射される。中心部は、水を温めたり、食べ物を調理できるほど熱くなる。トルコや中国のような国では、屋根に太陽熱温水器を設置する。これらは、中に水道管を通した金属とガラス製の箱だ。ガラスが熱をとらえて、金属が水道管に太陽光を反射して当て、温水を家の中に運ぶ仕組みだ。

　私たちは、シリコンでできている太陽電池と呼ばれる装置を使って、発電するのにも太陽光を利用できる。太陽光がシリコンに当たると、その中の粒子が動いて、電気が発生する。1つの太陽電池が多くの電力を作るわけではないので、太陽電池を集めて、大きな太陽光パネルを作るのだ。

1	環境
2	社会
3	環境
4	健康
5	｜Ｔ・テクノロジー
6	医学
7	環境
8	｜Ｔ・テクノロジー
9	教育
10	社会

語　彙　リ　ス　ト

☐ bright	形 明るい	☐ 形容詞 enough to do	熟 ～するほど 形容詞 だ
☐ sunlight	名 太陽光	☐ electricity	名 電気
☐ reach	動 ～に達する	☐ device	名 機器
☐ thermal	形 熱による	☐ solar cell	名 太陽電池
☐ material	名 材料	☐ be made of	熟 ～でできている
☐ cooker	名 調理器	☐ silicon	名 シリコン
☐ hit	動 当たる	☐ particle	名 粒子
☐ surface	名 表面	☐ put ～ together	熟 ～を集める
☐ reflect	動 反射する		

▶ 単語10回CHECK　1 ☐　2 ☐　3 ☐　4 ☐　5 ☐　6 ☐　7 ☐　8 ☐　9 ☐　10 ☐

[At the moment], the best solar cells can only use about 25 percent
　　　M　　the best solar cellsを指す　　　　S　　　　V　　　　　　　O

(of the sunlight that hits them), and they are an expensive way (to
　　M　　関係代名詞のthat　　the best solar cellsを指す　S　V　　　　C

produce electricity). But people are inventing better and cheaper
不定詞　形容詞的用法　　M　　　　S　　　V　better and cheaper solar cellsを指す

solar cells [all the time]. [In the future], we will use them
　　O　　　　　M　　　　　　M　　　　　S　　V　　O

[to do more and more things]. You can already buy solar lights, solar
不定詞 副詞的用法 結果　　M　　S　　　V　　　　　　O

radios, and small solar panels [for things like computers and
　　　　　　　　　　　　　　　　　M　　　　前置詞のlike「〜のような」

phones]. solar lights, solar radios, small
　　　　solar panelsの3つの接続

　　　　　　　　　　不定詞 副詞的用法 結果
We can use solar power [to travel] too. [In July 2010], Andre
　S　　V　　　O　　　M　　　M　　　　M　　　S

Borschberg flew a solar plane (called Solar Impulse) [for 26 hours]
　　　　　　V　　　O　　　過去分詞の名詞修飾　　M　　　　M

[before he stopped]. Power (for the four engines) came [from 12,000
　　　M　　　　　　　S　　　M　　the planeを指す　V　　　M

solar cells] (on the wings of the plane). It was able to fly [at night]
　　M　　　　　M　　　　　　　　　　S　　V　　　M

[because of batteries inside the plane which kept solar energy].
　　　　　　　　　　　M

There are also solar boats, and [in the future], there may even be
M　V　　M　　　S　　　　　　　M　　　　M　　　V

solar buses and trains. Moreover, every two years, [in the World
　　　S　　　　　　　M　　　　M　　　　M

Solar Challenge], cars (that are powered by solar energy) travel
　　　S　　　関係代名詞のthat　　M　　　　V

[over 3,000 kilometers] [in Australia]. The fastest cars can reach
　　　M　　　　　　　　M　　　　　S　　　V

speeds (of 100 kilometers per hour)!
　O　　　　M

今のところ、最高の太陽電池でも、それを照らす太陽光のおよそ25%しか使用できないので、太陽電池は、電気を生み出すにはお金がかかる方法だ。しかし、人間は常により優れて安価な太陽電池を発明しているところだ。将来、私たちはそれらを使ってますます多くのことができるだろう。すでにソーラーライト、太陽電池ラジオ、そしてコンピューターや電話のようなものに使われる小さな太陽光パネルを購入できる。

私たちは太陽光を使って移動もできる。2010年の7月に、アンドレ・ボーシュバーグはソーラーインパルスと呼ばれるソーラー航空機を、自分がとめるまで26時間飛ばした。4つのエンジンを動かす動力は、飛行機の両翼に取り付けた12,000の太陽電池から供給された。それは太陽光エネルギーを貯めておく機内のバッテリーのおかげで、夜間でも飛行することができた。ソーラーボートも存在するし、将来はソーラーバスやソーラートレインも出てくるかもしれない。さらに、2年ごとに開催されるワールド・ソーラー・チャレンジでは、太陽光発電を動力源とした車が、オーストラリアを3,000キロ以上移動する。最速の車は、時速100キロの速度に達することも可能だ！

☐ at the moment	熟	今のところ
☐ expensive	形	高価な
☐ invent	動	発明する
☐ fly	動	～を飛ばす
☐ wing	名	翼

☐ plane	名	飛行機
☐ because of	熟	～が原因で
☐ moreover	副	さらに
☐ every	形	～ごとに

▶ 単語10回CHECK 1 2 3 4 5 6 7 8 9 10

右側メニュー：
1 環境
2 社会
3 環境
4 健康
5 IT・テクノロジー
6 医学
7 環境
8 IT・テクノロジー
9 教育
10 社会

23

A Bright Future

The sunlight that reaches Earth in one hour has as much energy as all the power that people use in a year. But how can we get this energy and use it on earth?

'Solar' means 'coming from the sun', so when you use sunlight to make things hot, it is called solar thermal power. Many buildings use materials like glass and plastic to catch sunlight and warm the building. In Africa, people use solar cookers. When light hits the surface of the cooker, it is reflected into the middle. The middle becomes hot enough to heat water or cook food. In countries like Turkey and China, people put solar water heaters on their roofs. These are metal and glass boxes with water pipes in them. The glass catches heat and the metal reflects sunlight onto the water pipes, which carry the hot water down into the houses.

We can use sunlight to make electricity too, with devices called solar cells, which are made of silicon. When sunlight hits the silicon, particles inside it move, and this makes electricity. One solar cell does not produce much power, so we put the cells together to make big solar panels.

At the moment, the best solar cells can only use about 25 percent of the sunlight that hits them, and they are an expensive way to produce electricity. But people are inventing better and cheaper solar cells all the time. In the future, we will use them to do more and more things. You can already buy solar lights, solar radios, and small solar panels for things like computers and phones.

We can use solar power to travel too. In July 2010, Andre Borschberg flew a solar plane called Solar Impulse for 26 hours before he stopped. Power for the four engines came from 12,000 solar cells on the wings of the plane. It was able to fly at night because of batteries inside the plane which kept solar energy. There are also solar boats, and in the future, there may even be solar buses and trains. Moreover, every two years, in the World Solar Challenge, cars that are powered by solar energy travel over 3,000 kilometers in Australia. The fastest cars can reach speeds of 100 kilometers per hour!

▶ 音読10回CHECK 1 ☐ 2 ☐ 3 ☐ 4 ☐ 5 ☐ 6 ☐ 7 ☐ 8 ☐ 9 ☐ 10 ☐

1 環境
2 社会
3 環境
4 健康
5 IT・テクノロジー
6 医学
7 環境
8 IT・テクノロジー
9 教育
10 社会

背景知識が
広がるコラム

BACKGROUND KNOWLEDGE
エネルギー問題

　エネルギー問題は、大学受験のみならず、昨今の社会において、非常に重要なテーマです。現代のエネルギー源は、大きく分けると① **化石燃料（fossil fuel）**、② **原子力（nuclear power）**、③ **再生可能エネルギー（renewable energy）** の3種類です。

　① **化石燃料**とは、**石油、石炭、天然ガス**に代表されるものです。地質時代に堆積(たいせき)した動植物の死骸(しがい)が、長い年月をかけて変成され、化石となってエネルギー利用されている有機物のことをいいます。現代でも主力のエネルギー源ですが、**化石燃料の燃焼により二酸化炭素が放出されて、地球温暖化の一因となってしまいます。**同時に、**化石燃料の採掘量には限りがあり、現在の依存状態から脱する必要があります。**くしくも、1970年代のオイルショックにより、エネルギー源を石油に極端に依存することの危険性が浮き彫りになりました。それから50年もの間、国や民間企業も合わせて、新しいエネルギー源の開発に力を注いできました。

　続いて、② **原子力**は、パワーは強力なものの、いったん原子力発電所で事故が起きると、チェルノブイリ原発事故や福島第一原発事故に見られるように、**周辺の生態系に多大なダメージを与える**ため、使用には懸念点や強い反対があります。

　最後の③ **再生可能エネルギー**は、**太陽光発電、風力発電**などが挙げられます。**環境被害が少なく、枯渇(こかつ)することもない**ために、非常に注目度が高まっています。本問でも登場した**太陽光発電**は、**太陽光を太陽電池によって電力に変換する方式**で、コストが高いものの、強い電力を確保できるので、最も注目度が高まっています。

　風力発電は、**風の力でタービンを回して電気に変換する方式**です。環境被害は少ないですが、電力供給が不安定という欠点があります。

社 会

個人情報漏洩問題

別冊p.6／制限時間20分／392 words

解答

| 問1 | B | 問2 | A | 問3 | B | 問4 | A | 問5 | D |

問6　B

解説

問1

A　強く　　B　誤って　　C　ひどく　　D　綿密に

空所（　ア　）を含む文は、By doing so, a person may（　ア　）install "spyware ～.「そうすることで、人は（　ア　）スパイウェアをインストールするかもしれない」である。**By doing so**とは、「**不要なプログラムをダウンロードすることや添付ファイルを開くこと**」を意味する。よって、望んでではなくて、B accidentally「**誤って**」スパイウェアをインストールするだと文意が通じるので、正解は**B**。

問2

A　銀行口座　　　　　B　サイバー犯罪者
C　電機会社　　　　　D　コンピューター

空所（　イ　）を含む文は、**They can then use information to illegally withdraw money from（　イ　）**「**彼ら（サイバー犯罪者）は情報を利用して、違法に（　イ　）からお金を引き出す**」で、情報を利用してお金を引き出す場所なので、**A bank accounts**が正解。

問3

A　コンピューターへの危険のほとんどは日本かアメリカだ。
B　ハッカーは多くの国で活動している。
C　世界中の消費者が攻撃をしている最中だ。
D　人はコンピューターを使って、世界を攻撃している。

下線部（ウ）These attacks can come from anywhere in the world. は、These attacks と anywhere がポイントになる。

論理 POINT ❷　these ＋ 名詞 は抽象の目印

　these ＋ 名詞 の表現は**抽象表現の目印**で、**その前に具体的説明があります。**最初に具体的説明をいくつか続けて、these ＋ 名詞 で抽象化する働きです。

　本問の these attacks も、その前の「**ハッカーが行うクレジットカード情報の詐取等の一連の攻撃のこと**」を指すとわかる。続いて、anywhere に着目する。すると、下線部（ウ）は「**ハッカーが行う一連の攻撃は世界のどこからでもくる可能性がある**」となるので、**B The hackers work in many countries.** が正解となる。

語彙 POINT ❶　肯定文の any

　肯定文で any が使われると、「**どんな～でも**」の意味になります。**anytime**「どんな時でも」＝「いつでも」、**anyone**「どんな人でも」＝「誰でも」、**anywhere**「どんな場所でも」＝「どこでも」になるので、覚えておきましょう。

A　必要として　　B　内側に　　C　真実は　　D　困って

　空所（　エ　）を含む文は、**Now a great number of companies are（　エ　）of establishing more reliable security systems.**「**今や非常に多くの企業がより信頼できるセキュリティシステムを確立することを（　エ　）**」である。第3段落では、時系列順に、In 2011, ～.、In 2013, ～.、That same year, ～. Now ～.とハッカーによる攻撃を列挙しているので、（　エ　）には、**A in need**が入ると特定できる。**be in need of**で「**～を必要としている**」の意味の熟語。

筆者は（　　　　）と考えている。
A　コンピューターは昨今では使用するにはリスクがありすぎる
B　人は多くのクレジットカードを持つべきだ
C　スパイウェアをダウンロードすることがコンピューターを守る
D　人はメールを開くときに注意すべきだ

　第4段落第2文**When using a computer, it is a good idea not to open any emails sent from unknown people.**「**コンピューターを使う際に、知らない人から送られてきたメールを開かないのはよい考えだ**」から、**D people should be careful when opening emails**が正解。

構文 POINT❶　接続詞の後ろのS be 省略

（例文）
When in school, you must observe the school rules.
🔑 学校にいる時は、その校則を守らなければならない。
　whenやifなどの従属接続詞は、**後ろのSとVが省略される**ことがあります。Sは**主節と同じSか一般人を表すyou**など、Vは**be動詞**が省略されます。例文では、whenの後ろに主節のSであるyouとareが省略されています。

　第4段落第2文では、**Whenの後ろに一般人を表すyouとare**、選択肢のDはwhenの後ろに**peopleの代名詞theyとare**が省略されている。

28

問6

第２段落第２文 They can then use information to illegally withdraw money from bank accounts, get credit card numbers, or create Internet accounts in someone's name.「彼らは情報を利用して、違法に銀行口座からお金を引き出したり、クレジットカード番号を入手したり、人の名前でインターネットの口座を開設したりしてしまう」から、**B ハッカーは盗んだ情報を利用してクレジットカード番号を盗んだり、他人名義のインターネットアカウントを作ったりする**が正解。

Aは、第１段落第３文 This happens when someone is tricked into downloading an unwanted program from a website or opening a file attached to an email. に反する。Cは本文に記述なし。Dは第４段落第６文・第７文に取引業者のパソコンがハッキングされる記述はあるが、「**すぐにクレジットカードを解約し**」との記述はないので不適。

Identity theft is a growing problem [for anyone who goes online].
S　　　　V　　　C　　　　　　　　　　　　M

People used to worry about this crime [only after their purse or
S　　　V　　　　　　　O　　　　　　　　　　　　M
identity theftを指す　　　　　　「～してようやく」

wallet was stolen], but today (an increasing number of) people are
　　　　　　　　　　　M　　　　　　　　　　　　　M　　　　S　　V
online identity theftを指す　　　　M

victims (of online identity theft). This happens [when someone is
C　　　　　M　　　　　　　　　S　　V　　　　　M

tricked into downloading an unwanted program from a website or
ウェブサイト上の望ましくないプログラムをダウンロードすることや、メールに添付されたファイルを開くこと

opening a file attached to an email]. [By doing so], a person may
　　　　　　過去分詞の名詞修飾　　　　　　　M　　　　　　S　　　V

accidentally install "spyware," a computer program that can access
　　　　　　　　　　O　　同格のカンマ　　　　　O'　　関係代名詞のthat

his or her address book, bank account information, credit card

numbers, user names and passwords.

The spyware secretly reports personal information [back to the
S　　　　M　　　V　　　　O　　　　　　　　　M

criminal hackers]. They can then use information [to illegally
the criminal hackersを指す　V　　　O　　不定詞 副詞的用法 結果

withdraw money from bank accounts, get credit card numbers, or
M　　　　　　　　　　　　　　　withdraw ～, get ～, create ～の3つの接続

create Internet accounts in someone's name]. Information may even
S　　　　V

be sold [to others who want to use it for illegal purposes].
　　　　　M　　　　　　　informationを指す

Criminal hackers also sometimes use computer attachments [to
S　　　　　M　　　M　　V　　　O　　criminal hackersを指す

break into the websites of large companies]. Then they steal the
不定詞 副詞的用法 結果　　　M　　　　　　　M　S　V　O

credit card information (of the customers). These attacks can come
　　　　　　　　　　　　M　　　　　　　　S　　　V

[from anywhere in the world].　ハッカーが行うクレジットカード
M　　　　　　　　　　　　　　情報の詐取等の一連の攻撃のこと

　個人情報の盗難は、インターネットを使う人なら誰にでも関係がある、深刻化している問題だ。人々は、以前は自分のハンドバッグや財布が盗まれてからようやく、この犯罪を心配したものだったが、今日では、ネット上での個人情報の盗難の犠牲者がますます増えている。これは、誰かが騙されてウェブサイト上の望ましくないプログラムをダウンロードしたり、メールに添付されたファイルを開いたりするときに起きる。そうすることで、住所録、銀行口座情報、クレジットカード番号、ユーザーネーム、そしてパスワードにアクセスできるコンピュータープログラムである「スパイウェア」を、誤ってインストールしてしまうかもしれない。

　スパイウェアは、秘密裏に個人情報をサイバー犯罪者に報告する。そして、彼らは情報を利用して、違法に銀行口座からお金を引き出したり、クレジットカード番号を入手したり、人の名前でインターネットの口座を開設したりしてしまう。情報は、それを違法な目的で利用したい人に売られることさえあるかもしれない。

　サイバー犯罪者は、時にコンピューターの添付ファイルを使って、大企業のウェブサイトに不正アクセスすることもある。それから彼らは顧客のクレジットカード情報を盗む。こうした攻撃は、世界中のどこからでもくる可能性がある。

1	環境
2	社会
3	環境
4	健康
5	IT・テクノロジー
6	医学
7	環境
8	IT・テクノロジー
9	教育
10	社会

語 彙 リ ス ト

☐ identity theft	名	個人情報の盗難		☐ accidentally	副	誤って
☐ used to do	助	以前は〜した		☐ bank account	名	銀行口座
☐ crime	名	犯罪		☐ secretly	副	密（ひそ）かに
☐ purse	名	ハンドバッグ		☐ hacker	名	ハッカー
☐ wallet	名	財布		☐ illegally	副	違法に
☐ a number of	熟	たくさんの〜		☐ withdraw	動	引き出す
☐ victim	名	被害者		☐ purpose	名	目的
☐ be tricked into doing	熟	騙されて〜する		☐ attachment	名	添付ファイル
☐ unwanted	形	望ましくない		☐ break into	熟	侵入する
☐ attach A to B	動	AをBに取り付ける		☐ customer	名	顧客

▶ 単語10回CHECK　1 ☐　2 ☐　3 ☐　4 ☐　5 ☐　6 ☐　7 ☐　8 ☐　9 ☐　10 ☐

[In 2011], a major Japanese electronics company reported ⟨that
M　　　　　　　　S　　　　　　　　　　　　　　V　名詞節の that
information was stolen through the company's online services⟩. The
　　O　　　　　　　　　　　　　　　　　　　　　　　　　　　　S
hackers got the user names, passwords and birth dates ⟨of 100
　　　　V　　O　the user names, passwords, birth dates の3つの接続　M
million users⟩. [In 2013], hackers stole the credit card information
　　　　　　　　　M　　　　　S　　　V　　　　　O
⟨of 40 million users of a large American department store
　　　　　　　　　　　　　M
chain⟩. That same year, a Japanese Internet company said ⟨that
　　　　　M　　　　　　　　　S　　　　　　　　　V　名詞節の that
information of 22 million customers might have been stolen⟩. Now
　　　　　　　　　　　　　　　　　　　　　　　　　　　　　　M
⟨a great number of⟩ companies are in need of ⟨establishing more
　　　M　　　　　　　　S　　　V　　　　　　動名詞　　O
reliable security systems⟩. Recently, [in 2017], ⟨hundreds of
　　　　　　　　　　　　　　　　M　　　　M　　　　M
thousands of⟩ computer users ⟨in over 150 countries⟩ lost access ⟨to
　　　　　　　　S　　　　　　　　　M　　　　　　V　　O　　M
their data⟩ [because of the "WannaCry virus"]."
　M

Still, there are things ⟨that people can do to protect themselves⟩.
M　　M　　V　S　形式主語　M　不定詞 副詞的用法
[When using a computer], it is a good idea ⟨not to open any emails
you are の省略　　　M　　S V　　形式主語　C　不定詞 名詞的用法　S′
sent from unknown people⟩. It is also important ⟨to delete spam
過去分詞の名詞修飾　　　　S V　M　　C　不定詞 名詞的用法　S′
messages right away and never open junk email⟩. One should avoid
　　　　　　　　　　　　　　　　　　　一般人を表す S　　V
⟨downloading software from websites you cannot trust⟩, and
動名詞　　　　　O　　　　関係代名詞の省略
everyone should have the most recent updates ⟨for their operating
S　　　V　　　O　　　　　　　M
systems⟩. [When using a public computer], it pays ⟨to be extra
you are の省略　　　M　　S V　不定詞 名詞的用法
careful⟩.
S′

2011年に、日本のある主要な電機会社が、会社のオンラインサービスを通じて情報が盗まれたと報告した。ハッカーは、1億人のユーザーのユーザーネーム、パスワード、生年月日を引き出した。2013年には、ハッカーがアメリカの大手デパートチェーンの4000万人のユーザーのクレジットカード情報を盗んだ。その同じ年に、日本のあるインターネット企業が、2,200万人の顧客の情報が盗まれたかもしれないと述べた。今や非常に多くの企業がより信頼できるセキュリティシステムの確立を必要としている。最近では、2017年に、「ワナクライウイルス」が原因で、150以上の国の数十万のコンピューターユーザーがそのデータへのアクセスができなくなった。

　そうであっても、自分を守るためにやれることがある。コンピューターを使う際に、知らない人から送られてきたメールを開かないのはよい考えだ。また、スパムメッセージはすぐに削除して、迷惑メールを決して開かないことも重要だ。信頼できるウェブサイトからのソフトウェアのダウンロードを避けて、みんながOSを最も新しいものに更新すべきだ。公共のコンピューターを使うときは、さらに注意したほうがよい。

electronics	名	電子機器	access	名	アクセス
birth date	名	生年月日	protect	動	守る
a number of	熟	たくさんの〜	delete	動	削除する
be in need of	熟	〜を必要とする	right away	熟	すぐに
establish	動	確立する	junk mail	名	迷惑メール
reliable	形	信頼できる	update	名	更新
recently	副	最近	pay	動	割に合う

▶ 単語10回CHECK　1　2　3　4　5　6　7　8　9　10

右側の欄:

1 環境
2 社会
3 環境
4 健康
5 IT・テクノロジー
6 医学
7 環境
8 IT・テクノロジー
9 教育
10 社会

[If you discover a company you do business with has been hacked],
M　　名詞節のthatの省略　　関係代名詞の省略（you ～ with まで関係詞節）

a companyを主語とするV▼

the best idea is 〈to change your user name and password
S　　　　V　　不定詞 名詞的用法　　　　　　　　　　　C

immediately〉. Also, watch all credit card activity closely and report
　　　　　　　　M　　V　　　　O　　　　　　M　　　V

anything unusual [to the card company].
　　O　　　　　　M

本文訳

もし仕事で関係のある会社がハッキングされたとわかったら、最もよい考えは、ユーザーネームとパスワードをすぐに変えることだ。また、すべてのクレジットカードの動きをしっかりと見て、おかしなことは何でもカード会社に報告すること。

語彙リスト

☐ immediately	副 すぐに	☐ unusual	形 異常な
☐ closely	副 綿密に		

▶ 単語10回CHECK 1 ☐ 2 ☐ 3 ☐ 4 ☐ 5 ☐ 6 ☐ 7 ☐ 8 ☐ 9 ☐ 10 ☐

Identity theft is a growing problem for anyone who goes online. People used to worry about this crime only after their purse or wallet was stolen, but today an increasing number of people are victims of online identity theft. This happens when someone is tricked into downloading an unwanted program from a website or opening a file attached to an email. By doing so, a person may accidentally install "spyware," a computer program that can access his or her address book, bank account information, credit card numbers, user names and passwords.

The spyware secretly reports personal information back to the criminal hackers. They can then use information to illegally withdraw money from bank accounts, get credit card numbers, or create Internet accounts in someone's name. Information may even be sold to others who want to use it for illegal purposes.

Criminal hackers also sometimes use computer attachments to break into the websites of large companies. Then they steal the credit card information of the customers. These attacks can come from anywhere in the world. In 2011, a major Japanese electronics company reported that information was stolen through the company's online services. The hackers got the user names, passwords and birth dates of 100 million users. In 2013, hackers stole the credit card information of 40 million users of a large American department store chain. That same year, a Japanese Internet company said that information of 22 million customers might have been stolen. Now a great number of companies are in need of establishing more reliable security systems. Recently, in 2017, hundreds of thousands of computer users in over 150 countries lost access to their data because of the "WannaCry virus."

Still, there are things that people can do to protect themselves. When using a computer, it is a good idea not to open any emails sent from unknown people. It is also important to delete spam messages right away and never open junk email. One should avoid downloading software from websites you cannot trust, and everyone should have the most recent updates for their operating systems. When using a public computer, it pays to be extra careful. If you discover a company you do business with has been hacked, the best idea is to change your user name and password immediately. Also, watch all credit card activity closely and report anything unusual to the card company.

▶音読10回CHECK 1 ☐ 2 ☐ 3 ☐ 4 ☐ 5 ☐ 6 ☐ 7 ☐ 8 ☐ 9 ☐ 10 ☐

背景知識が
広がるコラム

BACKGROUND KNOWLEDGE
Identity theft

Identity theft（個人情報窃盗）とは、主にインターネットを介して他人の個人情報を入手して悪用する犯罪です。コンピューターをウイルスに感染させて、そこから住所氏名、電話番号、生年月日、クレジットカード番号などが詐取されてしまいます。

では、どうやってこの**個人情報窃盗**を防ぐか。本文にあったように、まずは**メールの添付ファイルを開くときやアプリをダウンロードするときに、細心の注意を払います**。知らない人からのメールは削除して、添付ファイルは絶対に開かない。アプリは、**信頼のおけないものや、不特定多数のアプリを使用しない**といった対策をとるとよいでしょう。

特に、**メール上に書かれているリンクを不用意にクリックしない**ようにします。リンクには**マルウェアという不正かつ有害な動作を行う意図で作成された、悪意のあるソフトウェアが含まれている可能性**があります。それから、**フィッシングサイト**という、本物のサイトを装った偽物のサイトがあります。パスワードやIDなどの認証情報を入力してしまうと、フィッシングサイトの所有者に利用されてしまいます。

他にも、**ウイルス対策ソフトを使用して、自分のパソコンや携帯電話を守ること**が挙げられます。個人情報窃盗の多くは、ウイルス感染から情報を抜き取られるので、ウイルス感染に早期に気付いて、ウイルスを取り除くことができれば、1つの対策になるでしょう。

さらに、公共のWi-Fiネットワークは安全性に不安があるので、なるべく使用を避けて、**不特定多数が使用できない安全なWi-Fiネットワークを使用する**ようにしましょう。

1 環境
2 社会
3 環境
4 健康
5 IT・テクノロジー
6 医学
7 環境
8 IT・テクノロジー
9 教育
10 社会

プラスチックごみによる海洋汚染

別冊 p.10／制限時間25分／400 words

解答

問1 ロ　　問2 イ　　問3 イ　　問4 ハ

問5 ロ　　問6 ハ

問7 **実は、私たちは単に多く作っているだけではなく、毎年より多くを作っているのだ。**

解説

問1

第1段落によると、プラスチックの生産は（　　　）。

イ　ゆっくりと継続している　　ロ　加速している

ハ　減り続けている　　二　同じままだ

第1段落第1文 Mass production of plastics, which began just six decades ago, **has increased so rapidly**「プラスチックの大量生産は、ほんの60年前に始まったものだが、**急速に増加した**」から、ロ **speeded up** が正解。

問2

第1段落によると、科学者はプラスチックの量が（　　　）ので、ショックを受けた。

イ　とても多い　　　　　　ロ　特定するのが難しい

ハ　非常に多様な　　　　　二　計算が難しい

第1段落第2文 Even the scientists who set out to conduct the world's first calculation of how much plastic has been produced, ～, were surprised **by the size of the numbers.**「どれほどの量のプラスチックが生産され、～かを世界で最初に計測し始めた科学者ですら、**その数字の大きさに驚いた**」、**同段落第3文** a rapid and extreme **increase** in plastic production「プラスチックの生産が急速に極端に

増えていること」より、**イ so large** が正解。

1 環境
2 社会
3 環境
4 健康
5 Ｉ・Ｔ・テクノロジー
6 医学
7 環境
8 Ｉ・Ｔ・テクノロジー
9 教育
10 社会

> **問3**
>
> 第2段落によると、2050年までには、（　　　）。
> イ　海の中は魚よりもプラスチックのほうが多くなるだろう
> ロ　魚の消費が減るだろう
> ハ　海の中はプラスチックがより少なくなるだろう
> ニ　プラスチックの使用が減るだろう

　問題のリード文の2050をチェックすると、**第2段落第2文の by mid-century が今世紀の中ごろで2050年を指す**ので、該当箇所だとわかる。**The prediction that by mid-century, the oceans will contain more plastic waste than fish** has become one of the most-quoted statistics 〜.「**今世紀半ばまでには、海の中は魚よりもプラスチックごみのほうが多くなるだろう**という予測は、最も引用されている統計の1つとなった」より、**イ more plastic will be in the oceans than fish** が正解。この that は**同格の that** で、fish までの意味のカタマリを作り、**The prediction の説明**をするはたらきがあることに注意する。

> **問4**
>
> 第2段落によると、およそ5億7千万メートルトンのプラスチックが（　　　）。
> イ　処分されている　　　ロ　焼却されている
> ハ　再利用されている　　ニ　埋められている

　問題のリード文の570 million metric tons of plastic に着目する。**第2段落第5文 Of that, only nine percent has been recycled.** の that が前文のプラスチックごみの63億メートルトンを指す。63億メートルトンの9%はおよそ5億7千万メートルトンなので、**ハ recycled** が正解。

第3段落によると、15年ごとに、（　　　）の量が2倍になる。
　イ　プラスチック技術　　　ロ　生産されたプラスチック
　ハ　プラスチック汚染　　　ニ　再利用されたプラスチック

　問いのリード文にある **every 15 years**「**15年ごとに**」をスキャニングして、**第3段落第5文 The rapid growth of plastic manufacturing, which so far has doubled approximately every 15 years, ～.** に着目する。plastic manufacturing「プラスチック製造の量」が2倍になっているとわかるので、**ロ plastic produced** が正解。

解法 POINT ❶　スキャニング

　内容一致問題は、問題文のリード文を先読みしますが、その中で**特定の用語に着目して、本文での該当箇所を特定する技術をスキャニング**といいます。スキャニングする表現は、**固有名詞、数字、使用頻度の低い単語**など、問題の該当箇所を見つけるのが容易になる表現です。

　い who を関係代名詞と考えると、**人にあたる先行詞が必要**になる。**う engineer** が唯一それに該当して、空所の手前の an environmental の後ろに置くことで、「**環境工学者**」となる。who の後ろには動詞を持ってきて、**specializes in**「**～を専門にする**」とする。目的語に動名詞の studying を使って、plastic waste「プラスチックごみ」を続けて完成。完成した英文は an environmental（**engineer who specializes in studying plastic**）waste in the oceans「海洋プラスチックごみの研究を専門にする環境工学者」となる。よって、2番目に **い who**、5番目に **か studying** がくるので、**ハ**が正解。

| 1 環境 |
| 2 社会 |
| 3 環境 |
| 4 健康 |
| 5 IT・テクノロジー |
| 6 医学 |
| 7 環境 |
| 8 IT・テクノロジー |
| 9 教育 |
| 10 社会 |

問7

構文図解

It's not just that we make a lot, it's that we also make more,
　　　　　　　　　 S　 V　　 O　　　　　　　　 S　 M　　 V　　 O

year after year.
　　　 M

構文 POINT ❷ **It is that ～ .の構文**

（例文）

It is that I have two daughters.

訳 実は、私には2人の娘がいる。

It is that ～ . で、「**実は～**」という構文があります。それに加えて、**not just A（but）also B**「**AだけではなくBも**」が使われていて、「**実は、単にAであるだけではなく、Bだ**」となります。

あてはめると、「**実は、私たちは単に多く作っているだけではなく、毎年より多くを作っているのだ**」が正解になる。

Here's ⟨How Much Plastic Trash is Littering the Earth⟩
　　　　M　V　S　「どれほどの量の〜か」

(1) Mass production ⟨of plastics⟩, [which began just six decades
　　　　　　S　　　　　　M　　　▼「(そして) それは」

ago], has increased so rapidly [that it has created 8.3 billion metric
　　　　V　　　　　M　　　▼ mass production of plastics を指す　　M
　　　　　　　　　　　　　　　so 〜 that... 「とても〜なので…」

tons — most of it in disposable products that end up as trash]. Even
　　　　　　　8.3 billion metric tons　M　　関係代名詞の that　　　　S

the scientists ⟨who set out to conduct the world's first calculation of
　　　　　　　　　　　　　　　　　M

how much plastic has been produced, disposed, burned or put in
　「どれほど多くのプラスチックが〜か」　　produced, disposed, burned, put の接続

landfills⟩, were surprised [by the size of the numbers]. "We all knew
　　　　　　　V　　　　　　　M　　　　　名詞節の that の省略

there was a rapid and extreme increase in plastic production from
　　　　　　　　　　　　O

1950 until now, but actually quantifying the number for all plastic
　　　　　動名詞 (quantifying 〜 made が was quite shocking に対する S)

ever made was quite shocking," says Jenna Jambeck, an environmental
　　　　　　　　　　　　　　　V　　S　　　　同格のカンマ
　過去分詞の名詞修飾

engineer who specializes in studying plastic waste in the oceans.
　関係代名詞の who、先行詞は an environmental engineer　　　　S'

(2) The study was launched [two years ago] [as scientists tried to
　　　S　　　V　　　　M　　　　　M

measure the huge amount of plastic that ends up in the seas and the

harm it is causing to birds, marine animals, and fish]. The prediction
　　　▼ plastic を指す　　　　関係代名詞の that　　　　　　　　S
　関係詞の省略

⟨that by mid-century, the oceans will contain more plastic waste
　同格の that　　　　　　M

than fish⟩ has become one ⟨of the most-quoted statistics⟩ and a
　　　　　　V　　C　　　　　M　　　　　　　one と a rallying cry
　　　　　　　　　　　　　　　　　　　　　　の接続

rallying cry ⟨to do something about it⟩.
　C　　　　　　　M　　　プラスチックごみ
　　不定詞
　　形容詞的用法

どれほどの量のプラスチックごみが地球を汚しているか

（1）プラスチックの大量生産は、ほんの60年前に始まったものだが、急速に増加したので、83億メートルトンを生み出し、そのほとんどが最終的にごみになる使い捨ての製品に使われている。どれほどの量のプラスチックが生産され、処分され、焼却され、埋立地に入れられたりしてきたかを世界で最初に計測し始めた科学者ですら、その数字の大きさに驚いた。「私たちはみな、1950年から今までに、プラスチックの生産が急速に、極端に増えていることをわかっていたが、実際に今まで作られたすべてのプラスチックの量を計算すると、かなり衝撃的だった」と、海洋プラスチックごみの研究を専門にする環境工学者のジェナ・ジャムベックは言う。

（2）その研究は、科学者が最終的に海に流れ込むプラスチックの膨大な量と、それが鳥、海洋生物、魚に与える害を計測しようと、2年前に始まった。今世紀半ばまでに、海の中は魚よりもプラスチックごみのほうが多くなるだろうという予測は、最も引用されている統計の1つとなり、その問題について何かをすべきだというスローガンとなった。

☐ trash	名 ごみ		☐ quantify	動 計る
☐ litter	動 ～を汚す		☐ specialize in	熟 ～を専門にする
☐ mass	形 大量の		☐ launch	動 始める
☐ rapidly	副 迅速に		☐ measure	動 計測する
☐ disposable	形 使い捨ての		☐ harm	名 害
☐ end up	熟 最終的に～になる		☐ marine	形 海の
☐ set out to do	熟 ～し始める		☐ prediction	名 予測
☐ conduct	動 行う		☐ contain	動 含んでいる
☐ calculation	名 計算		☐ quote	動 引用する
☐ landfill	名 埋立地		☐ rallying cry	名 ときの声、スローガン
☐ extreme	形 極端な			

▶ 単語10回CHECK 1 2 3 4 5 6 7 8 9 10

1 環境
2 社会
3 環境
4 健康
5 IT・テクノロジー
6 医学
7 環境
8 IT・テクノロジー
9 教育
10 社会

The new study, [published in the journal Science Advances], is the
S　　　　　　　分詞構文　　　　　　　　　M　　　　　　　　V　C

first global analysis (of all plastics ever made ― and their fate). [Of
M　　　　　　　　　　　　　　　　　　　　　　　　　M

関係代名詞の that　　　　　M　　　過去分詞の名詞修飾

the 8.3 billion metric tons that has been produced], 6.3 billion metric

63億メートルトンのプラスチックごみ　S

tons has become plastic waste. [Of that], only nine percent has been
V　　　　　C　　　　　M　　　　　　S　　　　　　　　V

recycled. The vast majority ― 79 percent ― is accumulating [in
S　　　　　　　S′　　　　　　　　V　　　　M

landfills] or ending up [in the natural environment] [as waste].
V　　　　　　　M　　　　　　　　M

(3) Roland Geyer, the study's lead author, says ⟨the team of
S　　　同格のカンマ　　　　S′　　　　　V　名詞節の that の省略

scientists are trying to create a foundation for better managing
O

plastic products⟩. "You can't manage what you don't measure," he
O　　　　　関係代名詞の what　　　　　S

says. "It's not just that we make a lot, it's that we also make more,
V　　「単に～ではない」　　　　　　　　　O

year after year." Half the resins and fibers used in plastics were
O　　　　　過去分詞の名詞修飾

produced in the last 13 years, the study found. The rapid growth (of
S　　　　V　　　　　S　　　　M

plastic manufacturing), (which so far has doubled approximately
「(そして) それは」　　　　　　M

every 15 years), has outpaced nearly every other artificial material.
V　　　　　　　O

プラスチックを指す

And, it is [unlike virtually every other material]. Half (of all steel
S　V　　　　　M　　　　　　　　　　S　　　M

produced), for example, is used [in construction], [with a decades-
過去分詞の名詞修飾　　M　　V　　　　M　　　　　M

long lifespan]. Plastic takes more than 400 years [to degrade],
S　　V　　　　O　　不定詞 副詞的用法　M

plastic を指す

so most (of it) still exists [in some form]. Half of all plastic
S　　M　　M　V　　　M　　　　　　O

manufactured becomes trash in less than a year, the study found.
過去分詞の名詞修飾　　　　　　　　　　S　　　V

その新しい研究は、サイエンス・アドバンス誌で公表されたが、今までに作られたすべてのプラスチック製品とその運命の最初の世界的な分析である。製造された83億メートルトンのうち、63億メートルトンがプラスチックごみとなっている。その中で、9％しか再利用されていない。79％もの膨大な量が、埋立地で蓄積されているか、ごみとして自然環境に放置されている。

(3) その研究の*筆頭著者であるローランド・ガイヤーは、科学者のチームが、プラスチック製品をよりしっかりと管理するための基礎を作ろうとしていると述べている。「人は計測できないものを管理できない」と彼は言う。「実は、私たちは単に多く作っているだけでなく、毎年より多くを作っているのだ」と続ける。プラスチックで使われる樹脂や繊維の半分がここ13年のうちに作られことが、その研究でわかった。プラスチック製造の急速な増加は、今までおよそ15年ごとに倍になっており、他のほぼすべての人工物のペースをしのぐ勢いだ。また、プラスチックは、他のほぼすべての物質と異なる。例えば、製造されるすべての鉄鋼の半分は、建設業に数十年単位の寿命で使用される。プラスチックは、分解するのに400年以上かかるので、そのほとんどが何らかの形でいまだに残っている。製造されたすべてのプラスチックの半分が、1年以下でごみになると、その研究で判明した。

*「筆頭著者」とは、著者が複数いるときに一番初めに名前が書かれる、中心的な人物を指す。

publish	動 公表する	manufacturing	名 製造
global	形 世界全体の	so far	熟 今まで
analysis	名 分析	outpace	動 追い越す
fate	名 運命	nearly	副 ほぼ
recycle	動 再利用する	artificial	形 人工の
vast	形 膨大な	material	名 素材
majority	名 大多数	unlike	前 ～と違って
accumulate	動 蓄積する	virtually	副 ほぼ
foundation	名 基礎	steel	名 鉄鋼
manage	動 管理する	construction	名 建設
year after year	熟 毎年	lifespan	名 寿命
resin	名 樹脂	degrade	動 分解する
fiber	名 繊維		

▶ 単語10回CHECK　1　2　3　4　5　6　7　8　9　10

右側欄外:
1 環境
2 社会
3 環境
4 健康
5 ＩＴ・テクノロジー
6 医学
7 環境
8 ＩＴ・テクノロジー
9 教育
10 社会

Here's How Much Plastic Trash is Littering the Earth

(1) Mass production of plastics, which began just six decades ago, has increased so rapidly that it has created 8.3 billion metric tons — most of it in disposable products that end up as trash. Even the scientists who set out to conduct the world's first calculation of how much plastic has been produced, disposed, burned or put in landfills, were surprised by the size of the numbers. "We all knew there was a rapid and extreme increase in plastic production from 1950 until now, but actually quantifying the number for all plastic ever made was quite shocking," says Jenna Jambeck, an environmental engineer who specializes in studying plastic waste in the oceans.

(2) The study was launched two years ago as scientists tried to measure the huge amount of plastic that ends up in the seas and the harm it is causing to birds, marine animals, and fish. The prediction that by mid-century, the oceans will contain more plastic waste than fish has become one of the most-quoted statistics and a rallying cry to do something about it. The new study, published in the journal Science Advances, is the first global analysis of all plastics ever made — and their fate. Of the 8.3 billion metric tons that has been produced, 6.3 billion metric tons has become plastic waste. Of that, only nine percent has been recycled. The vast majority — 79 percent — is accumulating in landfills or ending up in the natural environment as waste.

(3) Roland Geyer, the study's lead author, says the team of scientists are trying to create a foundation for better managing plastic products. "You can't manage what you don't measure," he says. "It's not just that we make a lot, it's that we also make more, year after year." Half the resins and fibers used in plastics were produced in the last 13 years, the study found. The rapid growth of plastic manufacturing, which so far has doubled approximately every 15 years, has outpaced nearly every other artificial material. And, it is unlike virtually every other material. Half of all steel produced, for example, is used in construction, with a decades-long lifespan. Plastic takes more than 400 years to degrade, so most of it still exists in some form. Half of all plastic manufactured becomes trash in less

than a year, the study found.

▶ 音読10回CHECK 1 2 3 4 5 6 7 8 9 10

1 環境

2 社会

3 環境

4 健康

5 IT・テクノロジー

6 医学

7 環境

8 IT・テクノロジー

9 教育

10 社会

背景知識が広がるコラム

BACKGROUND KNOWLEDGE
プラスチックごみ問題の3R

『**大学入試　レベル別英語長文問題ソリューション2　ハイレベル**』の第1問でも、この**プラスチックごみ**の問題を扱いました。本当に入試頻出の英文なので、しっかりと理解しておきましょう。前回はその問題に関するコラムだったので、今回はその対策に焦点を当てて説明します。

プラスチックごみ問題への有効な対策は、頭文字をとって3Rと言われています。*Reduce*（リデュース「ごみを減らす」）、*Reuse*（リユース「繰り返し使う」）、*Recycle*（リサイクル「再利用する」）です。*Reduce*とは、具体的には、**ペットボトル飲料の購入を控えること**、そして買い物には**マイバッグを持参**して、**プラスチックごみの代表例であるゴミ袋を使わないこと**です。世界レベルで見ると、レジ袋の使用規制は、40を超える国で採用、もしくは、議会承認を受けており、課税・有料化を決めた国を含めると60か国に上ります。日本も2020年にレジ袋有料化がスタートしました。

2つめの*Reuse*（リユース）とは、**使えるものを繰り返し使うこと**です。例えば、**シャンプーや洗剤などは詰め替え用の製品を選ぶ**ことです。シャンプーや洗剤の容器もプラスチックでできているので、その容器を必要以上に消費することをおさえることができます。

最後の*Recycle*（リサイクル）とは、**ごみを資源として再び利用すること**です。再利用で大切なのは、ごみを正しく分別することに加えて、ごみを再生して作られた製品を利用することです。

民間企業においても、スターバックスの取り組みが、ニュースで取り上げられたことがあります。**プラスチック製のストローを紙ストローに替えて**、続いて**プラスチックカップも紙カップに切り替える**動きがあるようです。個人的にも、**プラスチック製のレジ袋が有料化**されたことで、ライフスタイルが少しずつ変わってきたように思います。

47

健康

菜食主義

別冊 p.14 ／制限時間20分／ 360 words

解答

1. C **2.** A **3.** B **4.** C **5.** A

解説

文章を読んで、それぞれ最も適した選択肢を選びなさい。

1.

次のうち、ベジタリアンになる理由として挙げられていないのはどれか。

A. もっと健康になりたい人がいる。
B. 貧しすぎて肉を買えない人がいる。
C. 抗生物質やホルモン剤を効率よく摂取したい人がいる。
D. 動物に残酷なことをしたくない人がいる。

論理 POINT ❸ 複数名詞は抽象の目印

複数名詞は抽象表現の目印になることがあります。特に、**段落1行目の後半によく登場する**ので、覚えておきましょう。この**抽象表現**に気付くと、後ろに**具体例が続く**とわかるので、「例えば」という言葉を補って、見えない文のつながりを見抜きます。

　本問では、第1段落第1文の**many reasons**に着目する。「**多くの理由**」と言われて、「**多くの理由とは何だろう?**」と反応する。後ろから、その具体例が始まる。followingの後ろのコロン（:）を「例えば」と読み換えると、抽象と具体のつながりに気付く。

| 1 環境 |
| 2 社会 |
| 3 環境 |
| 4 健康 |
| 5 ITテクノロジー |
| 6 医学 |
| 7 環境 |
| 8 ITテクノロジー |
| 9 教育 |
| 10 社会 |

論理 POINT ❹ 3つ以上の並列は具体例の目印

英語では、**3つ以上の情報が並列**されていると、**具体例の目印**になります。情報の並列が始まる前に、「**例えば**」と補って、**見えない文のつながりを見抜き**ましょう。

本問では、第1段落第1文後半から、health, religious convictions, concerns ～, or a desire to ～と**4つの名詞が並列**されているので、**具体例の目印**になる。その4つは前のmany reasonsの具体例と理解すると、文と文のつながりが完璧に見えてくる。要は、「**人がベジタリアンになる多くの理由**」が抽象表現で、その具体例が「**健康、宗教上の信念、また、動物福祉や家畜への抗生物質、ホルモン剤の使用に対する懸念、過度な環境資源の利用を避ける方法で食事をしたいと望むこと**」になる。

上記の説明より、**第1段落第1文**で、**health**「健康」、**concerns about animal welfare**「動物福祉に対する懸念」が挙げられているので、AとDを正解の候補から外す。ちなみに、「動物福祉」とは、人間が動物に対して与えるマイナスを最小限に抑えて、動物の幸福を実現する考えのことをいう。

さらに、**第1段落第2文Some people follow a largely vegetarian diet because they can't afford to eat meat.**「肉を食べる経済的余裕がないから、大部分をベジタリアン食にする人もいる」より、Bも正解の候補から外す。

よって、**C**が正解になる。**第1段落第1文にconcerns about animal welfare or the use of antibiotics and hormones in farm animals**「動物福祉や家畜への抗生物質、ホルモン剤の使用に対する懸念」とあり、これは**抗生物質やホルモン剤という健康によくない物質を避けたいという内容**で、Cと反するのでCが正解になる。このように、**NOT問題は消去法で解く**ことを覚えておく。

解法 POINT ❷ NOT問題は消去法で

1のような**NOT問題**は、選択肢を1つずつ本文と照らし合わせて、**消去法で残った選択肢が正解**となります。

次のうち、この文章での世論調査による報告はどれか。

A. アメリカで多様な種類のベジタリアン食を実践する人の数

B. 人がベジタリアンになる理由

C. ベジタリアン食の健康上のメリットに関する統計上の情報

D. ベジタリアンリソースグループが菜食主義を広めるためにどんな
   貢献をしたか

poll「**世論調査**」は使用頻度がさほど高くない単語なので、スキャニングの対象となり、本文の**第2段落第1文**の該当箇所が容易に発見できる。同段落にpoll「世論調査」の報告内容が記載されており、**同段落第1文** Approximately six to eight million adults in the United States eat no meat, fish, or poultry「アメリカではおよそ600万〜800万人の成人が、肉、魚、家禽類（かきんるい）を食べない」、同段落第2文 Several million more have eliminated red meat but still eat chicken or fish.「さらに数百万人が赤身の肉を避けるが、鶏肉や魚は食べる」、同段落第3文 About two million have become vegans「およそ200万人がビーガンだ」から、**A**が正解。

ちなみに、ビーガンとは乳製品や卵すら食べない厳格なベジタリアンのことで、家禽類とは卵などの目的で家で飼うニワトリなどを指す。

3.

第3段落は何を示しているか。

A. 人はベジタリアン食が大きな栄養上のメリットがある可能性を昔から信じてきた。

B. ベジタリアン食は、栄養が適切である限り、有益になりうる。

C. ベジタリアン食は、すべての病気を予防できるが、一部の病気は治すことができない。

D. ビーガン食は、最近栄養に欠陥があると認識されている。

論理 POINT ❺ 時の対比

英語では「**昔は~だったが、今は…**」という時の対比は、頻出の論理展開です。以下に**時の対比の目印になる表現**を紹介します。
used to do「**以前は~だった(今は違う)**」／ **in the past**「その昔」
~ ago「~前」／ **traditionally**「従来は」／ **now**「今は」
nowadays「今日は(昔と違って)」

本問では、第3段落第1文の**Traditionally**に着目する。「従来は」と言われて、「**では今はどうなのか?**」と反応する。同じ文の後半にある**but in recent years**で時の対比に気付く。本文では「**昔は菜食主義の研究は栄養不足の可能性に焦点が当てられてきたが、近年は肉食を避ける健康上のメリットを確認している**」という内容。ちなみに、次の文の**Nowadays**も時の対比を表す単語で、「昔と違って今日は」というニュアンスが込められている。

上記の時の対比に気付くと、**第3段落第3文** "appropriately planned vegetarian diets, including ~ , are healthy, nutritionally adequate「(~を含めて)きちんと計画されたベジタリアン食は、健康的で栄養面も適切」** から、**B**が正解かつ**D**は不適。不正解の選択肢を見ていくと、Aは**have always believed**「昔から信じてきた」から、不適。**always**は言い過ぎで、誤りの選択肢を作るのによく使われる。

Cは、**can prevent all illnesses**「すべての病気を予防できる」が言い過ぎで、第3段落最終文 the prevention and treatment of **certain diseases**「一定の病気の予防や治療」に反するので、不適。**all も言い過ぎ**で、誤りの選択肢を作るのによく使われる。

この文章によると、「きちんと計画されたベジタリアン食」に関する次の説明のうち正しいのはどれか。

- A. 植物性食品にこだわる限り、体重が増える可能性は低い。
- B. ソーダ、チーズピザ、そしてキャンディは肉が入っていないので、健康に悪くない。
- C. 自分がどんな種類の油や脂肪を摂取しているかに注意すべきだ。
- D. 食料を選ぶとき、カロリーではなくて、栄養価にのみ注意すべきだ。

第4段落第5文 It's also vital to replace some harmful types of fats with good fats, such as those found in nuts and olive oil.「また、いくつかの有害な脂肪をナッツやオリーブオイルに含まれる良質な脂肪に換えることもきわめて重要だ」から、Cが正解。

不正解の選択肢を見ていくと、同段落第6文 And always keep in mind that if you eat too many calories, even from nutritious, low-fat, plant-based foods, you'll gain weight.「そして、もし栄養のある低脂肪の植物性食品でも、カロリーをとりすぎたら、体重が増えると、常に心に留めておくこと」より、Aは不適。

同段落第3文 A diet of soda, cheese pizza, and candy, after all, is technically "vegetarian."「ソーダ、チーズピザ、キャンディのような食事は、結局定義上は、『ベジタリアン食』となってしまう」は、3つの情報が並列されていることからも、具体例の目印になる。前文の「ベジタリアンになることが必ずしも健康にいいわけではない」の具体例なので、Bは不適。Dは本文に記述なし。**only は言い過ぎ**で、誤りの選択肢によく使われることに注意する。

1 環境

2 社会

3 環境

4 健康

5 ｜Ｔ・テクノロジー

6 医学

7 環境

8 ｜Ｔ・テクノロジー

9 教育

10 社会

5.

この文章によると、次の説明のうち正しいのはどれか。

A. 菜食主義が人気の理由の一部は、今はベジタリアン用の外食メニューがより豊富にあるからだ。

B. 肉食を避ける食文化はいまだに少数派なので、菜食主義の人気にまったく影響がない。

C. ビーガンは新鮮な時だけ肉を食べるので、病気になる可能性が低い。

D. 一度ベジタリアンになると、運動不足を心配しなくてもいい。

第1段落最終文 **Becoming a vegetarian has become more appealing and accessible, thanks to the all-year availability of fresh produce, more vegetarian options for eating out, and the growing influence of cultures with largely plant-based diets.** 「1年中新鮮な農作物が手に入る、**外食先でより多くのベジタリアンのメニューがある**こと、そして、ほとんどが植物由来で作られる食文化の影響が増えているおかげで、ベジタリアンになることは、より魅力的で身近になっている」より、**A**が正解。**produce** は**名詞**で使われると「**農作物**」の意味になるので注意する。

不正解の選択肢を見ていくと、上記の第1段落最終文より、もはや少数派ではないので B は不適。C は**第2段落第3文**、**~ vegans, who are people who avoid not only animal flesh ~**「**動物の肉だけでなく~も避けるビーガン**」に反するので不適。ちなみに C の **fresh**「**新鮮な**」と同文の **flesh**「**肉**」は別の単語なので注意する。

D は**第4段落最終文 So it's also important to practice portion control, read food labels, and engage in regular physical activity.**「**だから、食べる量をコントロールして、食品の表示を読み、定期的に体を動かすことも重要だ**」に反するので**不適**。

People become vegetarians [for many reasons], (including the
　　　S　　　　V　　　　　C　　　　　　　M　　　　　　「～を含んで」　　M
following: health, religious convictions, concerns about animal
　　　　　　　　　　health, religious convictions, concerns ~ animals, a desire ~ の接続
welfare or the use of antibiotics and hormones in farm animals, or a
animal welfare と the use of ~の接続　　　　antibiotics と hormones の接続
desire to eat in a way that avoids excessive use of environmental
　　　　　　　　　　　　関係代名詞のthat
resources). Some people follow a largely vegetarian diet [because
　　　　　　　　　S　　　　V　　　　　　　　O　　　　　　　M
they can't afford to eat meat]. 〈Becoming a vegetarian〉 has become
　　　some people を指す　　　　　　動名詞　　　　S　　　　　V
more appealing and accessible, [thanks to the all-year availability of
　　　　　　　C　　　　　　　　　　　　　　M
fresh produce, more vegetarian options for eating out, and the
　　　the all-year availability ~ , more vegetarian ~ , the growing influence ~ diets の接続
growing influence of cultures with largely plant-based diets].

Approximately six to eight million adults (in the United States)
　　　　　　　　　　　　S　　　　　　　　　　　　　M
eat no meat, fish, or poultry, [according to a Harris Interactive
V　　　　O　　　　　　　　　　　　　　　M
poll conducted by the Vegetarian Resource Group, a nonprofit
　　　過去分詞の名詞修飾　　　　　　　　　　　　　　同格のカンマ
organization that spreads information about vegetarianism]. Several
　　　　　　　関係代名詞のthat　　　　　　　　　　　　　　　　　S
million more have eliminated red meat but still eat chicken or fish.
　　　　　　V　　　　　　O　　　　M　　V　　　O
About two million have become vegans, (who are people who avoid
　　　S　　　　　　V　　　　C　「(そして)その人たちは」　M　　関係代名詞
not only animal flesh but also animal-based products such as milk,
not only A but also B「A だけではなく B も」　　　　　　B such as A「A のような B」
cheese, and eggs).

　人は次のことを含む多くの理由でベジタリアンになる。健康、宗教上の信念、また*動物福祉や家畜への抗生物質、ホルモン剤の使用に対する懸念、あるいは環境資源の過度の使用を避ける方法で食事をしたいという願いなどだ。肉を食べる経済的余裕がないという理由で、大部分をベジタリアン食にする人もいる。一年中新鮮な農作物が手に入る、外食先でより多くのベジタリアンのメニューがあること、そして、ほとんどが植物由来の食文化の影響が増えているおかげで、ベジタリアンになることは、より魅力的で身近になっている。

　菜食主義に関する情報を広めているNPO法人のベジタリアンリソースグループが行ったハリスインタラクティブ世論調査によると、アメリカではおよそ600万〜800万人の成人が、肉、魚、*家禽類（かきんるい）を食べない。さらに数百万人は赤身の肉を避けるが、鶏肉や魚は食べる。およそ200万人が動物の肉だけでなく、牛乳、チーズ、卵のような動物性食品を避けるビーガンだ。

*「動物福祉」とは、人間が動物に対して与えるマイナスを最小限にすることで、動物の幸福を実現する考えのことをいう。
*「家禽類」とは、肉や卵などをとる目的で、家で飼うニワトリなどの鳥類のこと。

reason	名 理由		accessible	形 近づきやすい
including	前 〜を含んで		thanks to	熟 〜のおかげで
following	名 次のもの		availability	名 手に入ること
religious	形 宗教の		produce	名 農作物
conviction	名 信念		option	名 選択肢
concern	名 心配		influence	名 影響
welfare	名 福祉		approximately	副 およそ
antibiotics	名 抗生物質		million	形 百万の
hormone	名 ホルモン		poultry	名 家禽類
desire	名 望み		according to	熟 〜によると
avoid	動 避ける		poll	名 世論調査
excessive	形 過度の		organization	名 組織
environmental	形 環境の		spread	動 広める
resource	名 資源		eliminate	動 削除する
diet	名 食事		flesh	名 肉
can't afford to do	熟 〜する余裕がない		product	名 製品
appealing	形 魅力的な		such as	熟 〜のような

▶ 単語10回CHECK　1　2　3　4　5　6　7　8　9　10

Traditionally, research (into vegetarianism) focused mainly on
   M   S   M   V

potential nutritional deficiencies, but [in recent years], studies are
             O   M   S   V

confirming the health benefits (of meat-free eating). Nowadays,
             O   M   M

plant-based eating is recognized [as not only nutritionally sufficient
      S   V ▼ a way to do「〜する方法」   M

but also as a way to reduce the risk for many chronic illnesses].
   ▲
   not only A but also B「A だけではなく B も」

[According to the American Dietetic Association], "appropriately
                         M   S

planned vegetarian diets, (including total vegetarian or vegan diets),
                       ▲   ▲
           「〜を含んで」   M   同格の or「すなわち」

are healthy, nutritionally adequate, and may provide health benefits
 V   C   V   O

[in the prevention and treatment of certain diseases]."
                      M

1 環境
2 社会
3 環境
4 健康
5 IT・テクノロジー
6 医学
7 環境
8 IT・テクノロジー
9 教育
10 社会

本文訳

　従来から、菜食主義に関する研究は、主に栄養不足の可能性に焦点が当てられてきたが、近年、研究によって、肉を食べないことの健康上のメリットが確認されつつある。今日では、植物性食品が中心の食事をすることは、栄養面でも十分であるだけではなく、多くの*慢性的な病気のリスクを減らす方法として認識されている。米国栄養士協会によると、「完全なベジタリアンであるビーガン食も含めて、きちんと計画されたベジタリアン食は、健康的で栄養面も適切で、一定の病気の予防や治療において、健康面のメリットをもたらしてくれるかもしれない」とのことだ。

*「慢性的」とは、症状が長引いて治りにくい病気の性質のことをいう。

語彙リスト

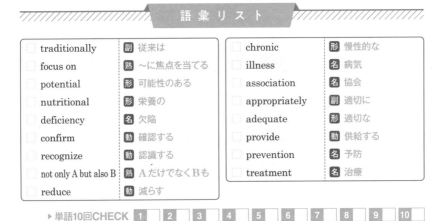

☐ traditionally	副 従来は		☐ chronic	形 慢性的な
☐ focus on	熟 ～に焦点を当てる		☐ illness	名 病気
☐ potential	形 可能性のある		☐ association	名 協会
☐ nutritional	形 栄養の		☐ appropriately	副 適切に
☐ deficiency	名 欠陥		☐ adequate	形 適切な
☐ confirm	動 確認する		☐ provide	動 供給する
☐ recognize	動 認識する		☐ prevention	名 予防
☐ not only A but also B	熟 A だけでなく B も		☐ treatment	名 治療
☐ reduce	動 減らす			

▶ 単語10回CHECK　1 ☐　2 ☐　3 ☐　4 ☐　5 ☐　6 ☐　7 ☐　8 ☐　9 ☐　10 ☐

"Appropriately planned" is the key term. [Unless you follow
　　　　　　　S　　　　　　V　　　　　C　　　　　　　　M
recommended guidelines on nutrition, fat consumption, and weight
　　　　　　　　　　　　　　　　　　　　　　　　▲
　　　　　　　　　　　　nutrition, fat consumption, weight controlの3つの接続
control], 〈becoming a vegetarian〉 won't necessarily be good [for
　　　　　　　　　　　　　　　▲
動名詞「〜すること」　S　　　not necessarily「必ずしも〜なわけではない」　V　　C　　M
you]. A diet 〈of soda, cheese pizza, and candy〉, [after all], is
　　　S　　　　　　　M　　　　　　　　　　　▼形式主語のit　　　　M　　　　V
technically "vegetarian." [For health], it's important 〈to make sure
　　　　▼名詞節のthat　　　　C　　　　M　　　S V　　C　　不定詞 名詞的用法　S′
that you eat a wide variety of fruits, vegetables, and whole grains〉.

　　▼形式主語のit
It's also vital 〈to replace some harmful types of fats with good fats,
S V　M　　C　　不定詞 名詞的用法　　　S′　　　replace A with B「AをBと取りかえる」
such as those found in nuts and olive oil〉. And always keep in mind
　　　　　　　　　　　　　　　　　　　　　　　　　　M　　　　V
　　　fatsを指す　　過去分詞の名詞修飾
〈that if you eat too many calories, even from nutritious, low-fat,
名詞節のthat　　　　　　　　　　　　　O
　　　　　　　　　　　　　　　　　　　　▼形式主語のit
plant-based foods, you'll gain weight〉. So it's also important
　　　　　　　　　　　　　　　　　　　　　　　S V　M　　　　C
〈to practice portion control, read food labels, and engage in regular
不定詞 名詞的用法　　　　　　　S′　　　practice 〜, read 〜, engage 〜の3つの接続
physical activity〉.

　「きちんと計画された」というのが重要な条件だ。栄養、脂肪の摂取、そして体重管理の推奨されているガイドラインに従わない限り、ベジタリアンになることは、必ずしもよいわけではないだろう。ソーダ、チーズピザ、キャンディのような食事は、結局定義上は、「ベジタリアン食」である。健康のためには、多様な果物、野菜、*全粒穀物を食べるように気を付けることが重要だ。また、いくつかの有害な脂肪をナッツやオリーブオイルに含まれる良質の脂肪に置き換えることもきわめて重要だ。そして、もし栄養のある低脂肪の植物性食品でも、カロリーをとりすぎれば、体重が増えると常に心に留めておくこと。だから、食べる量をコントロールして、食品の表示を読み、定期的に体を動かすことも重要だ。

*「全粒穀物」は、人間が主食にする小麦などを粉にする際、表皮などを取り除かずに作ったもので、栄養価が高いことで知られている。

☐ key	形 重要な		☐ replace A with B	動 AをBと取りかえる
☐ term	名 条件		☐ harmful	形 有害な
☐ unless	接 ～しない限り		☐ keep in mind	熟 ～を心に留める
☐ recommend	動 推奨する		☐ gain weight	熟 体重が増える
☐ guideline	名 指針		☐ practice	動 実践する
☐ consumption	名 消費		☐ portion	名 料理の量
☐ after all	熟 結局		☐ label	名 表示
☐ technically	副 厳密には		☐ engage in	熟 従事する
☐ make sure that ~	熟 ～するように注意する		☐ regular	形 定期的な
☐ grain	名 穀物		☐ physical activity	名 身体活動
☐ vital	形 きわめて重要な			

▶ 単語10回CHECK　1　2　3　4　5　6　7　8　9　10

1 環境　2 社会　3 環境　4 健康　5 IT・テクノロジー　6 医学　7 環境　8 IT・テクノロジー　9 教育　10 社会

59

People become vegetarians for many reasons, including the following: health, religious convictions, concerns about animal welfare or the use of antibiotics and hormones in farm animals, or a desire to eat in a way that avoids excessive use of environmental resources. Some people follow a largely vegetarian diet because they can't afford to eat meat. Becoming a vegetarian has become more appealing and accessible, thanks to the all-year availability of fresh produce, more vegetarian options for eating out, and the growing influence of cultures with largely plant-based diets.

Approximately six to eight million adults in the United States eat no meat, fish, or poultry, according to a Harris Interactive poll conducted by the Vegetarian Resource Group, a nonprofit organization that spreads information about vegetarianism. Several million more have eliminated red meat but still eat chicken or fish. About two million have become vegans, who are people who avoid not only animal flesh but also animal-based products such as milk, cheese, and eggs.

Traditionally, research into vegetarianism focused mainly on potential nutritional deficiencies, but in recent years, studies are confirming the health benefits of meat-free eating. Nowadays, plant-based eating is recognized as not only nutritionally sufficient but also as a way to reduce the risk for many chronic illnesses. According to the American Dietetic Association, "appropriately planned vegetarian diets, including total vegetarian or vegan diets, are healthy, nutritionally adequate, and may provide health benefits in the prevention and treatment of certain diseases."

"Appropriately planned" is the key term. Unless you follow recommended guidelines on nutrition, fat consumption, and weight control, becoming a vegetarian won't necessarily be good for you. A diet of soda, cheese pizza, and candy, after all, is technically "vegetarian." For health, it's important to make sure that you eat a wide variety of fruits, vegetables, and whole grains. It's also vital to replace some harmful types of fats with good fats, such as those found in nuts and olive oil. And always keep in mind that if you eat too many calories, even from nutritious, low-fat, plant-based foods, you'll gain weight. So it's also important to practice portion control, read food labels, and engage in regular physical activity.

▶ 音読10回CHECK　1　2　3　4　5　6　7　8　9　10

1 環境
2 社会
3 環境
4 健康
5 ＩＴ・テクノロジー
6 医学
7 環境
8 ＩＴ・テクノロジー
9 教育
10 社会

背景知識が広がるコラム

BACKGROUND KNOWLEDGE
菜食主義の功罪

　自己流で行う**菜食主義の難点**は、**動物性たんぱく質の摂取を一切やめてしまうと、栄養不足になる可能性があること**です。特に、**ビタミンD不足と、ビタミンB12不足**が指摘されています。ビタミンDには、**骨の健康を保つ働きや、免疫力を高める働き**があります。よって、菜食主義でビタミンD不足になると、骨粗鬆症や骨折の危険性が高まる可能性があります。

　それから、特にコロナウイルスが蔓延している昨今では、**ビタミンDの栄養素に注目が集まっています。血中ビタミンD濃度が30ng/ml以上の人はコロナウイルスにほとんど感染せず、たとえ感染しても重症化しない**という論文が発表されました。菜食主義でビタミンDが不足すると、コロナウイルスのみならず、インフルエンザなどの感染症にかかりやすくなる可能性があります。

　続いて、菜食主義は、ビタミンB12不足になる恐れがあります。ビタミンB12の摂取量が減ると、**貧血になる可能性や記憶力や思考力の低下**などのリスクも高まります。そのために、菜食主義者は、ビタミンDやビタミンBをサプリメントで補う必要が指摘されています。

　一方で、菜食主義には、**内臓脂肪を減らす、心臓病やガン発生リスクの低下、動脈硬化や高血圧の予防**といったメリットもあります。常に、**功罪という観点**で、**物事のプラスとマイナスの視点を理解する姿勢**が重要です。

　個人のライフスタイルは尊重されるべきなので、**さまざまな食習慣があってよいもの**だと思います。実際に、私もいろいろな食事法を試してきました。自分の経験からは、**極端な食事法ではなく、バランスよく多くの栄養素を摂取すること**が、いちばん体によいのかと思います。

人工知能の功罪

解答

(問1) 1 A　　2 D　　3 B　　4 D　　5 A
　　　6 C　　7 C　　8 A　　9 B
(問2) 1 D　　2 A　　3 C　　4 A　　5 B

解説

(問1)

1

(A) 我慢する　　　　(B) 拒絶する
(C) 解放する　　　　(D) 欠けている

suffer from「～に苦しむ」は、**endure**「(苦痛など)を我慢する」と近いので、**(A)** が正解。

....

2

(A) プライドの源　　(B) 知識の源
(C) 愛情の源　　　　(D) 収入源

下線部(2)が含まれる文の **losing their jobs to automation**「オートメーションで仕事を失うこと」から、ロボットに盗まれるのは「収入源」とわかるので **(D) sources of income** が正解。**livelihood**は「生計の手段」の意味。

....

3

(A) 危険な　　　　　(B) 危機に瀕して
(C) 価値のある　　　(D) 厄介な

vulnerable「もろい」は、簡単な単語に置き換えると**weak**と同義。(B) **at risk**が最も近いので、これが正解。

(A) 予期された　　　　(B) 時間に正確な
(C) 活動的でない　　　(D) 迅速な

rapid「**迅速な**」は、(D) **swift**「**迅速な**」と同義なので、これが正解。

. . . .

(A) とにかく　　　　　(B) ぜひとも
(C) 望めば　　　　　　(D) 平均して

At any rate「**どんな割合でも**」＝「**とにかく**」から、(A) **Anyway**
が正解。(B) **By all means**は「**すべての手段を使っても**」＝「**ぜひとも**」
の意味で、**招待された際の返事などに使う表現**。

. . . .

(A) 計画する　　　　　(B) ふりをする
(C) 予期する　　　　　(D) 後悔する

predictは、**pre**「**前に**」＋ **dict**「**言う**」＝「**予言する**」から、(C)
anticipateが正解。

. . . .

(A) 不満な　　　　　　(B) 安定した
(C) 効果的な　　　　　(D) 思いやりのある

productive「**生産的な**」から、(C) **effective**が最も近いので、これ
が正解。

. . . .

(A) 気付くこと　　　　(B) 無視すること
(C) 考慮すること　　　(D) 記録すること

recognizing「**認識すること**」から、(A) **noticing**が最も近いので、
これが正解。

. . . .

1 環境
2 社会
3 環境
4 健康
5 IT・テクノロジー
6 医学
7 環境
8 IT・テクノロジー
9 教育
10 社会

（A）予防できる　　（B）避けられない
（C）不確実な　　　（D）衝動的な

inevitable「避けられない」から、（B）unavoidable が正解。

> ▶語彙 POINT ❷ in(un) は「否定」の意味
>
> 　単語の頭に in や un が付くと、「否定」の意味になることがあります。例えば、inevitable は、in「否定」＋ evit「避ける」＋ -able「～できる」＝「避けられない」となります。in には「～の中に」の意味に加えて、「否定」の意味があることを覚えておきましょう。他にも incredible ＝ in「否定」＋ credit「信頼する」＋ -ible「～できる」＝「信じられない」などがあります。

　本問では、（B）unavoidable ＝ un「否定」＋ avoid「避ける」＋ -able「～できる」＝「避けられない」の意味になる。（C）も un「否定」＋ certain「確かな」＝「不確実な」の意味。

. . . .

問2

1

第1段落によると、次のうち正しいのはどれか。
（A）ロボットを恐れるのは非合理的だ。
（B）人は日常作業を、もうやりたくない。
（C）ブルーカラーの労働者は、ロボットに関して大して心配していない。
（D）たくさんの人が将来仕事を失うかもしれない。

　第1段落第1文 Understandably, many workers today suffer from job anxiety.「現代の多くの労働者が仕事の不安に苦しんでいるのはもっともなことだ」、**同段落最終文** No wonder so many workers are so uneasy.「非常に多くの労働者がとても不安になるのも不思議ではない」より、**(D)** が正解。（A）はこの最終文に反する。（B）は本文に記述なし。（C）は**第1段落第3文** It's a legitimate worry, of course, and not just for blue-collar employees.「もちろん、それはもっともな心配事であり、ブルーカラーの労働者に限った話ではない」、つまりブルーカラーの労働者が仕事を失うことを恐れるのはもっともだという記述に反する。**ブルーカラー**とは、**肉体労働者**を意味する。

2

第2段落によると、次のうち正しいのはどれか。
（A）技術革新は、新しい雇用の機会を作り出す。
（B）人間の労働者は、今起きている変化に対処できない。
（C）よい仕事はやがて過去のものになるだろう。
（D）その昔、テクノロジーはめったに仕事を奪うことはなかった。

　第2段落第5文 But this only means that new, more interesting "human" jobs are being created.「しかし、これは新しくて、より面白い『人間の』仕事が作られることを意味しているに過ぎない」より、(A)が正解。but, however などのうしろには、筆者の主張がくるので注意する。this は「人類が長年機械による仕事の代替を経験していること」を指す。

　(B)は、**同段落最終文 At any rate, Feldstein believes that workers have the resilience it takes to "adjust positively to any changing technology."**「いずれにせよ、フェルドシュタインは、労働者が『変わりゆくいかなるテクノロジーにも前向きに適応していく』のに必要な柔軟性を持っていると信じている」に反する。(C)は、本文に記述なし。(D)は同段落第4文に反する。

第3段落によると、次のうち正しいのはどれか。
（A）人間の従業員とロボットは、別々のグループに分けられるだろう。
（B）人間はロボットと競争するために、「デジタル化」していくだろう。
（C）最近、多くの企業が人間の従業員をロボットのように働かせたがっている。
（D）企業は、従業員がどのように考えるかを統制しなければならない。

　第3段落第9文 Most managers, Hunt says, tend to expect workers to perform like machines.「ほとんどの経営者が、労働者が機械のように動くことを期待する傾向にあると、ハントは言う」より、**(C)**が正解。

1 環境
2 社会
3 環境
4 健康
5 IT・テクノロジー
6 医学
7 環境
8 IT・テクノロジー
9 教育
10 社会

> パラフレーズとは言い換えのことで、**内容一致問題では頻出**です。
> **本文の記述をパラフレーズして、選択肢**が作られます。

本問でも、本文中の**expect O to do**「Oに〜することを期待する」を（C）では**want O to do**「Oに〜してもらいたい」に、本文中の**workers**を（C）では**human employees**に、本文中の**perform like machines**を（C）では**work in a robotic way**にパラフレーズしていることに気付くと、容易に正解できる。

③の残りの選択肢を見ていくと、（A）は、**第3段落第3文 Instead, more and more, they will be teamed up with them.**「その代わりに、ますます、彼らはロボットと協働するだろう」に反する。（B）、（D）は本文に記述なし。

・・・

④

第4段落によると、次のうち正しいのはどれか。

（A）人間は他人の気持ちを理解することに関して、ロボットより優れている。

（B）多くのロボットがいる職場では、それらに周囲の事情を読むように要求するだろう。

（C）ロボットの思考は、たいていは人間にとって理解するには難しすぎる。

（D）ロボットは生きてはいないので、状況にしっかりと適応できる。

第4段落第3文 Humans excel at making emotional connections, scanning environments, and recognizing patterns.「人間は心のつながりを作り、周囲の状況を読み取り、パターンを認識するのに秀でている」より、（A）が正解。本文の **excel**「優れている」が（A）の **are better** に、本文の **making emotional connections** が（A）の **understanding the feelings of others** にパラフレーズされているのに気付くと、容易に正解できる。（B）〜（D）は本文に記述なし。

・・・

次のうち本文のタイトルに最もふさわしいのはどれか。

（A）職場でのロボットの歴史　　（B）仕事の未来
（C）ロボット：最高の労働者　　（D）機械のように働く

解法 POINT ❹　タイトル問題

　タイトル問題では、**本文の一部にしか記述がないもの、本文に記述がないものを消去法**で、正解の候補から外します。**残った選択肢を比較して、本文のより広範囲な部分をカバーしているものを正解**とします。

　本問でも、(A)のような「歴史」、(C)のようなロボットに対する一面的な賛美は記述なし。(D)は**第3段落第9文Most managers, Hunt says, tend to expect workers to perform like machines.**「ほとんどの経営者が、労働者が機械のように動くことを期待する傾向にあると、ハントは言う」という記述があるが、**第4段落で、それをやめるように言い、人間にはまだまだロボットができないたくさんのことがやれると言っている**ので不適。

　第1段落はAIの台頭への労働者の不安、第2段落は人間が適応できる力を備えていること、第3段落は人間がロボットに淘汰されることはなく、むしろロボットとの協働が生じること、第4段落は人間はまだまだロボットにやれないことができるので、ロボットとの協働が重要になることを説いていることから、**(B)が正解**になる。

1 環境
2 社会
3 環境
4 健康
5 IT・テクノロジー
6 医学
7 環境
8 IT・テクノロジー
9 教育
10 社会

1 Understandably, many workers today suffer from job anxiety.
They fear ⟨losing their jobs to automation⟩ and ⟨having robots "steal" their livelihoods⟩. It's a legitimate worry, [of course], and not just [for blue-collar employees]. Many white-collar jobs are vulnerable, too. Let's face it: AI and robots can do many routine jobs more efficiently and more cheaply [than human workers]. This makes massive layoffs a real possibility. No wonder so many workers are so uneasy.

2 But Martin Feldstein, an economics professor at Harvard, says, "Not to worry." Why? "Simply put: History. [For many years], we have been experiencing rapid technological change ⟨that substitutes machines and computers for individual workers⟩." But this only means ⟨that new, more interesting "human" jobs are being created⟩. [At any rate], Feldstein believes ⟨that workers have the resilience it takes to "adjust positively to any changing technology"⟩."

68

1 環境

2 社会

3 環境

4 健康

5 IT・テクノロジー

6 医学

7 環境

8 IT・テクノロジー

9 教育

10 社会

本文訳

1　現代の多くの労働者が、仕事の不安に苦しんでいるのはもっともなことだ。彼らは*オートメーションによって仕事を失うこと、そしてロボットに生計手段を「盗まれる」ことを恐れている。もちろん、それはもっともな心配事であり、*ブルーカラーの労働者に限った話ではない。多くの*ホワイトカラーの労働者の仕事も*脆弱なものだ。現実を見よう。AIとロボットは人間の労働者より、多くの日常作業をより効率よく、より安価に行うことができる。このおかげで、大量の解雇が現実的な可能性として浮上する。非常に多くの労働者がとても不安になるのも不思議ではない。

2　しかし、ハーバード大の経済学の教授であるマーティン・フェルドシュタインは、「心配無用だ」と言う。なぜか？「簡単に言うと、歴史が証明してくれる。長年、私たちは機械やコンピューターが個々の労働者の代わりをする急速な技術革新を経験している」。しかし、これは、新しくて、より面白い「人間の」仕事が作られることを意味しているに過ぎない。いずれにせよ、フェルドシュタインは、労働者が「変わりゆくいかなるテクノロジーにも前向きに適応していく」のに必要な柔軟性を持っていると信じている。

* 「オートメーション」は、機械を組み合わせて、製造工程の管理・作業などを自動的に処理するシステムのこと。
* 「**ブルーカラー**」は**肉体労働者**を意味し、「**ホワイトカラー**」は**頭脳労働者**を意味する。工場労働者などが着る作業服の青い襟と、事務労働者のワイシャツの白い襟から。
* 「脆弱」は、もろく弱いことを意味する。

語彙リスト

☐ understandably	副 もっともなことだが		☐ massive	形 大量の	
☐ suffer from	動 ～に苦しむ		☐ layoff	名 解雇	
☐ anxiety	名 不安		☐ no wonder	熟 ～は不思議ではない	
☐ lose A to B	熟 BのせいでAを失う		☐ uneasy	形 不安な	
☐ automation	名 オートメーション（自動化）		☐ economics	名 経済学	
☐ livelihood	名 生計の手段		☐ professor	名 教授	
☐ legitimate	形 もっともな		☐ simply put	熟 簡単に言うと	
☐ worry	名 心配事		☐ rapid	形 迅速な	
☐ blue-collar	形 ブルーカラーの		☐ technological	形 技術的な	
☐ employee	名 従業員		☐ substitute A for B	熟 Bの代わりにAを使う	
☐ white-collar	形 ホワイトカラーの		☐ at any rate	熟 いずれにせよ	
☐ vulnerable	形 脆弱な		☐ resilience	名 柔軟性	
☐ routine	形 日課の		☐ adjust	動 適応する	
☐ efficiently	副 効率よく		☐ positively	副 前向きに	

▶ 単語10回CHECK　1　2　3　4　5　6　7　8　9　10

3 Business experts don't expect large-scale unemployment to happen
either. They predict 〈that most workers won't actually be replaced
by robots〉. Instead, more and more, they will be teamed up [with
them]. What will that be like? How will human workers get
along with their machine partners? Dr. Steve Hunt, a business
psychologist and systems designer, believes 〈that "digitization" can,
paradoxically, create a more human, more productive workplace〉. But
this can only happen [if digitization is applied correctly]. Doing that,
he says, depends mainly on companies changing their mindset. Most
managers, Hunt says, tend to expect workers to perform like
machines. They judge employee performance [by "tangible,
immediate outcomes that measure the kind of output a machine
would produce]."

4 This must stop, says Hunt. "We are going to need more and more
workers 〈to do the things robots can't do well〉. Humans excel
[at making emotional connections, scanning environments, and
recognizing patterns]. They can then adapt their behavior to fit the
situation." Hunt cites research 〈that shows that human workers
almost always treat the robots they work with as living things〉.

3　ビジネスの専門家も、大規模な失業が起きるとは考えていない。彼らは、ほとんどの労働者が実際にはロボットで代替（だいたい）されないだろうと予言する。その代わりに、ますます、彼らはロボットと協働するだろう。それはどのようなものになるか。人間の労働者はどうやって、機械のパートナーとうまくやるのだろうか。経営心理学者でシステムデザイナーのスティーブ・ハントは、*「デジタル化」は逆説的に、より人間的で、より生産的な職場を作るだろうと考えている。しかし、これはデジタル化がきちんと適用された場合にのみ起こる。そのようになるには、主に、会社がその考え方を変えることにかかっていると、彼は言う。ほとんどの経営者が、労働者が機械のように動くことを期待する傾向にあると、ハントは言う。彼らは「機械が生み出す生産高といったものを評価するときの目に見える直接的な結果」で従業員の業績を判断する。

4　これをやめなければならないとハントは言う。「私たちはロボットがうまくやれないことをやれるますます多くの労働者を必要とするだろう。人間は心のつながりを作り、周囲の状況を読み取り、パターンを認識するのに秀でている。そして、その行動を、状況に合うように調整することができる」。ハントは、人間の労働者がほぼいつも協働するロボットを生き物とみなすことを示す研究を引用する。

*「デジタル化」は、人間が行っていることをコンピューターで表現すること。

expert	名 専門家	apply	動 適用する
expect O to do	熟 Oが～するのを予期する	correctly	副 正しく
large-scale	形 大規模の	depend on	動 ～にかかっている
unemployment	名 失業	mindset	名 考え方
predict	動 予言する	perform	動 動く
replace	動 ～に取ってかわる	tangible	形 具体的な、実体のある
instead	副 その代わりに	immediate	形 直接の
be teamed up with	熟 ～と協働する	outcome	名 結果
get along with	熟 ～とうまくやる	measure	動 ～を評価する
psychologist	名 心理学者	output	名 生産高
designer	名 設計者	excel	動 優れている
digitization	名 デジタル化	connection	名 つながり
paradoxically	副 逆説的に	scan	動 ざっと読み取る
productive	形 生産的な	fit	動 ～に合う
workplace	名 職場	cite	動 引用する

▶ 単語10回CHECK　1　2　3　4　5　6　7　8　9　10

1 環境
2 社会
3 環境
4 健康
5 IT・テクノロジー
6 医学
7 環境
8 IT・テクノロジー
9 教育
10 社会

人間の労働者が一緒に働くロボットを生き物とみなすこと

Companies must recognize this and incorporate this information
　　S　　　　　V　　　　　　O　　Companiesを指す　　V　　　　　O

[into their management policies]. They must prepare for the
　　　　　　　M　　　　　　　　　　S　　　V　　　　　O

inevitable social and psychological interactions (that will take place

関係代名詞の that　　M

between man and machine). Only then, says Hunt, will the "digitized
workplace を指す　　　　　　　　O　　　V　　S　　Only then が文頭に出たことによる倒置

workplace be one that we'll run towards and not away from."

関係代名詞の that

企業はこのことを認識して、この情報を経営方針に組み込まなければならない。企業は、人間と機械の間に起こる当然の社会的、心理的な*相互作用に備えなければならない。そのときにようやく「デジタル化された職場は、私たちがそこから逃げ出すところではなく、目指すべきところ」になるだろうとハントは言う。

*「相互作用」は、たがいに働きかけて影響を及ぼすことを意味する。

1 環境
2 社会
3 環境
4 健康
5 IT・テクノロジー
6 医学
7 環境
8 IT・テクノロジー
9 教育
10 社会

語 彙 リ ス ト

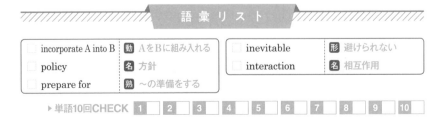

□ incorporate A into B	動 AをBに組み入れる		□ inevitable	形 避けられない
□ policy	名 方針		□ interaction	名 相互作用
□ prepare for	熟 ～の準備をする			

▶単語10回CHECK　1　2　3　4　5　6　7　8　9　10

1 Understandably, many workers today suffer from job anxiety. They fear losing their jobs to automation and having robots "steal" their livelihoods. It's a legitimate worry, of course, and not just for blue-collar employees. Many white-collar jobs are vulnerable, too. Let's face it: AI and robots can do many routine jobs more efficiently and more cheaply than human workers. This makes massive layoffs a real possibility. No wonder so many workers are so uneasy.

2 But Martin Feldstein, an economics professor at Harvard, says, "Not to worry." Why? "Simply put: History. For many years, we have been experiencing rapid technological change that substitutes machines and computers for individual workers." But this only means that new, more interesting "human" jobs are being created. At any rate, Feldstein believes that workers have the resilience it takes to "adjust positively to any changing technology."

3 Business experts don't expect large-scale unemployment to happen either. They predict that most workers won't actually be replaced by robots. Instead, more and more, they will be teamed up with them. What will that be like? How will human workers get along with their machine partners? Dr. Steve Hunt, a business psychologist and systems designer, believes that "digitization" can, paradoxically, create a more human, more productive workplace. But this can only happen if digitization is applied correctly. Doing that, he says, depends mainly on companies changing their mindset. Most managers, Hunt says, tend to expect workers to perform like machines. They judge employee performance by "tangible, immediate outcomes that measure the kind of output a machine would produce."

4 This must stop, says Hunt. "We are going to need more and more workers to do the things robots can't do well. Humans excel at making emotional connections, scanning environments, and recognizing patterns. They can then adapt their behavior to fit the situation." Hunt cites research that shows that human workers almost always treat the robots they work with as living things. Companies must recognize this and incorporate this information into their management policies. They must prepare for the inevitable social and psychological interactions that will take place between

man and machine. Only then, says Hunt, will the "digitized workplace be one that we'll run towards and not away from."

▶ 音読10回CHECK　1　2　3　4　5　6　7　8　9　10

1 環境
2 社会
3 環境
4 健康
5 ITテクノロジー
6 医学
7 環境
8 ITテクノロジー
9 教育
10 社会

BACKGROUND KNOWLEDGE
AIに奪われる仕事と残る仕事

背景知識が広がるコラム

昨今、AIに関連する論文は非常に多岐にわたるので、今回は**AIと仕事**という観点に限定します。例えば、イギリスのオックスフォード大学は、**近い将来に今ある仕事の90%はAIに置き換えられる**と公表しました。野村総合研究所は、**この先15年で現在の仕事の49%がなくなる**というレポートを発表しました。**AIに奪われる仕事の特徴として、単純計算・単純作業**が中心の仕事が挙げられます。**計算や計測などの仕事、機械的な作業や機械の操作・運転**なども、人が行うよりもAIが行うほうがスピードと正確性が増します。

上記の研究によると、例えば、一般事務、銀行員、警備員、コンビニの店員、タクシーや電車の運転手がAIに代替される仕事として挙げられています。実際に、コンビニでは**無人レジ**が多数導入されており、私も頻繁に利用します。タクシーや電車の運転手は、**自動運転車**の開発の影響を受けるでしょう。

一方で、**知性や判断、複雑な作業、コミュニケーションが要求される仕事**はAIに代替されにくいと考えられます。**芸術性や創作活動を伴う仕事、他の人が簡単には代わることのできない複雑な作業**、そして、**感情や思いやり、人と人との触れ合いが重視されるコミュニケーションを伴った仕事**です。

例えば、営業職、介護職、カウンセラーなどの人との触れ合いが重要で、コミュニケーション能力が求められる仕事は、AIに代替されにくい仕事として挙げられています。
私のまわりにも、大学でAI関連の研究をする友人たちが複数います。彼らに実際に話を聞くと、高度な専門性を伴う仕事ですら近い将来なくなる可能性があるとのことです。

まずは、**簡単には他の人にはできない、専門性を深めていくこと**が重要になります。そして、**人間ならではの知性や判断**を大切にします。そして、**仕事の細部に人間の最大の強みである感情や思いやりを込めて、1つ1つのコミュニケーションを大切にする**ことが、ますます求められていく世の中になるのでしょう。

牛乳の摂取と骨密度の関係

1. （1）D　　（3）B　　（4）A
2. C　　**3.** D　　**4.** A, C

解説

1.

（1）　示すこと
　A．調査すること　　B．見つけること
　C．抗議すること　　D．示すこと

　demonstrating「**示すこと**」と同義はD. **showing**。「**示す**」のパラフレーズは頻出なので注意する。

語彙 POINT ❸ 「示す」のパラフレーズ

　showがいちばん簡単な「**示す**」という意味の単語で、近い意味で **indicate, demonstrate, illustrate** などがあります。厳密に言うと、**indicate は show を少し堅くした言葉**で、**demonstrate は実際の例を見せて示す**、**illustrate は図表などを使って示す**というニュアンスがあります。

（3）　実際に
　A．訓練して　　B．実際に　　C．努力せずに　　D．準備せずに

　practiceには「**練習**」の意味の他に「**実際**」の意味があるので、**in practice**「**実際に**」から、**B. in reality** が正解。

（4）　捨てる

　A.　処分する　　B.　終える　　C.　減らす　　D.　投げる

pour「注ぐ」＋away「離れて」＝「捨てる」から、**A. dispose of** が正解。「**捨てる**」のパラフレーズも頻出なので、整理する。

> ▶**語彙 POINT ❹**「捨てる」のパラフレーズ
>
> 　**throw away** がいちばん簡単な「**捨てる**」という意味の単語で、近い意味で **discard, do away with, dispose of, pour away** などがあります。

2.

　A.　さらに　　B.　幸運なことに　　C.　明らかに　　D.　それゆえに

　第2段落第2文 The ideal study 〜 assign every member of one group to drink plenty of milk daily for several decades, while the other group would drink some kind of milk substitute instead. 「理想的な調査は〜、一方のグループの全員に数十年にわたって、たくさんの牛乳を毎日飲むことを割り当てる一方で、もう1つのグループには、牛乳の代わりとなるものを飲ませるものだろう」は、**理想的な**という表現からも、数十年にわたって毎日たくさんの牛乳を飲むような指示を出す実験は、「**明らかに**」実践するには難しすぎるので、**C. Obviously** が正解。

1 環境
2 社会
3 環境
4 健康
5 IT・テクノロジー
6 医学
7 環境
8 IT・テクノロジー
9 教育
10 社会

3.

A. 牛乳の摂取量が骨密度とどう関係しているかを調査する代わりの方法は、少なくとも10年間数千人の健康を追った後に、その人たちを調査することだ。

B. 問題は、いつも牛乳を飲む人の老化と骨密度の相関関係の可能性に関することだ。

C. 1997年に登場したハーバード大学の研究では、研究者は7万人以上の女性看護師の健康に、非常に感銘を受けた。

D. ハーバード大学の研究では、個人が摂取した牛乳の量は、腕や腰の骨折の頻度に大きな影響はなかった。

第4段落最終文 In that study, researchers found no significant difference in the numbers of broken arms or hips between people who drank one glass of milk a week or less and those who drank two or more. 「その研究では、週にコップ1杯かそれ以下しか牛乳を飲まない人と、週に2杯かそれ以上飲む人との間に、腕や腰の骨折の数で、研究者たちは有意な違いが発見できなかった」より、**D**が正解。In that study は、**同段落第1文**より「ハーバード大学の研究」とわかる。

不正解の選択肢を見ていくと、Aは**第3段落第1文と似ているが、ask them how much milk they've been drinking over the years**「数年にわたって、どれほどの牛乳を飲んできているかを尋ねて」が抜けているので不適。B、Cは本文に記述なし。

4.

A. 2014年の2つの後発の研究は、牛乳を平均以上に摂取することは、身体の健康にマイナスの影響を与えるかもしれないことを示唆すると報告されていた。

B. 私たちが牛乳に関してどういう行動を取るかを決めるには、定期的にどれほど牛乳を飲むかを正確に計測するまで待つべきだ。

C. 人がどれほどの牛乳を毎日、あるいは年単位で飲むかを推測する方法は明らかではない。

D. 明確な証拠がないので、牛乳を有難く思うと、それを飲むことを支持する証拠が増えることになる。

E. 牛乳を飲むのはおそらく骨によいことなのだが、より長生きできるかもしれない。

第5段落第1文 〜 , in 2014 came the results of two large Swedish studies which led to headlines that drinking more than three glasses of milk a day — a larger amount than most people drink — was no help to your bones, and might even harm you. 「2014年には、1日にコップ3杯以上というほとんどの人が飲むよりも多い量を飲むことは、骨にプラスにならないどころか、害を与えるかもしれないという見出しに結び付いた2つの大規模なスウェーデンの研究結果が出てきた」より、Aが正解。この文は、in 2014がM、cameがV、the resultsがSのMVSであることに注意する。

構文 POINT ❸ MVS

（例文）
At that place began my school life.
訳 あの場所から、私の学校生活が始まった。
　第1文型（SVM）が倒置されるとMVSになります。例文は、Atから前置詞句が始まり、placeまでの意味のカタマリを作りM、beganがV、my school lifeがSのMVSになります。

最終段落第2文、第3文 the people who took part were required to estimate their milk consumption during the previous years, which is no easy task. It's hard to know how much you eat with cereal, or in tea, or in cooking. は、要するに「シリアルや紅茶、料理などでどれほど牛乳を飲んでいるかがわからないので、牛乳の摂取量のおおよその計算をするのが難しい」ということなので、Cが正解。

Bは本文に記述なし。

Dは、最終段落第4文 the current weight of evidence suggests that it is still OK to continue to drink milk if you like it は、要は「好きならば牛乳を飲み続けても構わない」とあるだけで、「飲むことを支持する」とまでは言っていないので、不適。

Eは、最終段落最終文より、「おそらく骨によい」とは書いてあるが、「より長生きできる」とは書かれていないので不適。

1 環境
2 社会
3 環境
4 健康
5 IT・テクノロジー
6 医学
7 環境
8 IT・テクノロジー
9 教育
10 社会

[In many parts of the world], children are told to drink milk every
　　　　　　　M　　　　　　　　　　　　S　　　V　　▼tell O to do の受動態
　　　　　　　　　　　　　　　　　　　　　　　　　　　to do
day [because doing so will give them strong bones]. The idea does
　　　　　　　牛乳を飲むこと　 M　children を指す　骨が強くなるから毎日牛乳を飲むこと　 V

make some sense. Milk contains calcium, and calcium is known
　　　　　O　　　　S　　　V　　　　O　　　　　　S　　　　V
[to improve bone density].
　　　M

But ⟨demonstrating a definite link between milk consumption and
　　　動名詞　　　　　S　　　　　牛乳の摂取量と骨密度の明確なつながりを証明すること
bone density⟩ is more complex [than it sounds]. The ideal study
　　　　　　　　V　　　C　　　　　　　M　　　　　　　　S
would take two large groups (of people) and assign every member (of
　　V　　　　　O　　　　　　M　　　　　V　　　　O　　　　　M
one group) to drink plenty of milk daily for several decades, while the
　　　　　　to do
other group would drink (some kind of) milk substitute instead.
一方のグループに数十年単位で牛乳を毎日飲ませて,他方のグループに牛乳の代わりを飲ませる実験のこと M　　　　O　　　　M
Obviously, this is too difficult [to do in practice].
　　　　　　M　　S　V　　C　　　too ~ to...　M
⟨What we can do instead⟩ is ⟨to take thousands of people, ask
　関係代名詞の what　　S　　V　不定詞 名詞的用法　　　　C
them how much milk they've been drinking over the years, and then
　thousands of people を指す　　　　　　　take ~, ask ~, follow ~ の接続
follow them for at least a decade to see whether those who regularly
　　　　　　　　　　　不定詞 副詞的用法　who ~ milk までの関係詞節を作る
drink milk are any less likely to suffer from broken bones later in
whether 節の中の those に対する V
life⟩.
　　数千人の人に牛乳の摂取量を尋ねて、定期的に牛乳を飲む人が骨折する可能性を確認すること
This is ⟨what happened in an article published in 1997 by Harvard
S　V　関係代名詞の what　　　C　　過去分詞の名詞修飾
University researchers⟩. An impressive 77,000 female nurses were
　　　　　　　　　　　　　　　　　S　　　　　　　　V
followed [for 10 years].
　　　　　M

80

1 環境 / 2 社会 / 3 環境 / 4 健康 / 5 IT・テクノロジー / 6 医学 / 7 環境 / 8 IT・テクノロジー / 9 教育 / 10 社会

世界の多くの場所で、子供たちが毎日牛乳を飲むように言われるのは、牛乳を飲むと骨が強くなるからだ。その考えは、ある意味で理にかなっている。牛乳はカルシウムを含み、カルシウムは*骨密度を改善することで知られているからだ。

しかし、牛乳の摂取量と骨密度の明確なつながりを示すことは、思っているよりも複雑で難しい。理想的な調査は、2つの大きなグループに行うもので、最初のグループの全員に、数十年にわたってたくさんの牛乳を毎日飲むことを割り当てる一方で、もう一つのグループには、牛乳の代わりとなるものを飲ませるものだろう。明らかに、これは難しすぎて実践できない。

その代わりに私たちがやれることは、数千人の人に対して、数年にわたり、どれほどの牛乳を飲んでいたかを尋ねて、少なくとも10年その人たちを追跡して、定期的に牛乳を飲む人がのちの人生で骨折する可能性が低いかどうかを確かめることだ。

これは、ハーバード大学の研究者が1997年に公表した論文に書かれていた実験だ。実験に協力的な7万7千人の女性の看護師が10年間追跡調査された。

*「骨密度」とは、骨の強度を表す指標のひとつ。

英語	品詞	意味
make sense	熟	意味をなす
contain	動	含んでいる
bone density	名	骨密度
demonstrate	動	示す
consumption	名	摂取
complex	形	複雑な
ideal	形	理想的な
assign O to do	動	Oに~することを割り当てる
plenty of	熟	たくさんの~
decade	名	十年
substitute	名	代替品
obviously	副	明らかに
in practice	熟	実際には
regularly	副	定期的に
be likely to do	熟	~しそうだ
article	名	論文
publish	動	公表する
impressive	形	協力的な

▶ 単語10回CHECK 1 2 3 4 5 6 7 8 9 10

[In that study], researchers found no significant difference (in the
M　ハーバード大で行われた研究　S　　V　　　　　　　O　　　　　　　M
numbers of broken arms or hips) (between people who drank one
　　　　　　　　　　　　　　　　　　　　M　　　　　関係代名詞の who
glass of milk a week or less and those who drank two or more).
　　　　　　　　　　　　　　　　　peopleを受ける代名詞

　　[To confuse things further], [in 2014] came the results (of two
　　不定詞 副詞的用法　　　M　　　　M　　　V　　　S　　　　M
large Swedish studies which led to headlines that drinking more
　　　　　　　　　　　　　　　　　　　　　　　　同格の that
than three glasses of milk a day — a larger amount than most people

drink — was no help to your bones, and might even harm you).
drinking ～ a day の S に対応する V

　　But [before we pour away the milk], there are some important
　　　　　　　　　　　　　　M　　　　　　　M　V　　　S
things (to take into account). [For example], [in the Swedish
　　　　不定詞 形容詞的用法　M　　　M　　require O to do の受動態　　　M
studies], the people (who took part) were required [to estimate their
　　　　　S　　　M　　　　V　　　to do
milk consumption during the previous years], which is no easy task.
　　　　　　　　　　　　　　　　　　　　　　　V　C
　　　　形式主語の it　　　　　　「どれほど～か」
It's hard ⟨to know how much you eat with cereal, or in tea, or in
S V　C　　不定詞 名詞的用法　　　　　　　　S′
cooking⟩. So, [until we know more], the current weight (of evidence)
　　　　形式主語の it　　　　M　　　　　　S　　　　　M
suggests ⟨that it is still OK to continue to drink milk if you like it⟩.
milk を指す V　名詞節の that　　O　　不定詞 名詞的用法　　　milk を指す
It probably does have benefits [for bone health], [even though such
S　　M　　強調の助動詞 do　V　O　　　　M　　　　　M 牛乳が骨の健康
benefits are shorter-lived than you might have hoped].　　　にプラスになる
　　　　　　　　　　　　　　　　　　　　　　　　　　　　こと

82

その研究では、週にコップ1杯かそれ以下しか牛乳を飲まない人と、週に2杯かそれ以上飲む人との間に、腕や腰の骨折の数で、研究者たちは＊有意な違いが発見できなかった。

さらに混乱することに、2014年には、1日にコップ3杯以上というほとんどの人が飲むよりも多い量を飲むことは、骨にプラスにならないどころか、害を与えるかもしれないという見出しに結び付いた2つの大規模なスウェーデンの研究結果が出てきた。

しかし、牛乳を捨てる前に、私たちが考慮に入れるべき重要なことがいくつかある。例えば、スウェーデンの研究で、被験者が前の数年間の牛乳の摂取量を推測するように求められたが、まったく簡単な作業ではなかった。シリアル、紅茶、料理などで、どれほど牛乳を飲んでいるかを知ることは難しい。だから、私たちがもっと多くのことを知るまで、現在出ている証拠の比重は、好きなら牛乳を飲み続けてもよいということのほうにあるようだ。牛乳はおそらく、骨の健康にプラスの影響が実際にある。もっともそのような恩恵はあなたが願っているよりも、長くは続かない。

＊「有意な」は、統計上、偶然ではなく必然である可能性があると推測されることを意味する。

significant	形	重要な
those who	熟	～する人々
confuse	動	混乱させる
lead to	熟	～に結び付く
headline	名	見出し
harm	動	害を与える
pour away	熟	捨てる
take O into account	熟	Oを考慮する
take part	熟	参加する

be required to do	熟	～することが要求される
estimate	動	見積もる
previous	形	以前の
task	名	作業
current	形	現在の
weight	名	比重
evidence	名	証拠
suggest	動	示す
probably	副	おそらく

▶単語10回CHECK　1　2　3　4　5　6　7　8　9　10

1 環境
2 社会
3 環境
4 健康
5 IT・テクノロジー
6 医学
7 環境
8 IT・テクノロジー
9 教育
10 社会

In many parts of the world, children are told to drink milk every day because doing so will give them strong bones. The idea does make some sense. Milk contains calcium, and calcium is known to improve bone density.

But demonstrating a definite link between milk consumption and bone density is more complex than it sounds. The ideal study would take two large groups of people and assign every member of one group to drink plenty of milk daily for several decades, while the other group would drink some kind of milk substitute instead. Obviously, this is too difficult to do in practice.

What we can do instead is to take thousands of people, ask them how much milk they've been drinking over the years, and then follow them for at least a decade to see whether those who regularly drink milk are any less likely to suffer from broken bones later in life.

This is what happened in an article published in 1997 by Harvard University researchers. An impressive 77,000 female nurses were followed for 10 years. In that study, researchers found no significant difference in the numbers of broken arms or hips between people who drank one glass of milk a week or less and those who drank two or more.

To confuse things further, in 2014 came the results of two large Swedish studies which led to headlines that drinking more than three glasses of milk a day — a larger amount than most people drink — was no help to your bones, and might even harm you.

But before we pour away the milk, there are some important things to take into account. For example, in the Swedish studies, the people who took part were required to estimate their milk consumption during the previous years, which is no easy task. It's hard to know how much you eat with cereal, or in tea, or in cooking. So, until we know more, the current weight of evidence suggests that it is still OK to continue to drink milk if you like it. It probably does have benefits for bone health, even though such benefits are shorter-lived than you might have hoped.

too much of a good thing

　私が子供のころは、"背が高くなるには牛乳を飲め"という風潮があり、水代わりに毎日牛乳を飲んでいた記憶があります。当時は、牛乳の問題点など、世間的には何も指摘されていませんでした。実際に、**牛乳にはタンパク質、各種ビタミン、カルシウムに代表されるミネラルなどの豊富な栄養**が含まれています。

　しかし、昨今では**牛乳はいろいろな病気を引き起こす可能性**が指摘されており、**花粉症やアトピーに代表される各種アレルギー、乳がんや前立腺がん、心臓病などのリスクを高める危険性**も指摘されています。

　それからもう一点、**乳糖不耐症**という問題が指摘されています。日本人は95%以上が**乳糖不耐症**と言われ、牛乳に含まれる乳糖を消化する酵素ラクターゼを持っていないために、下痢になったり、腸にガスが溜まりやすくなると言われています。

　最後に、牛乳に関しても功罪という視点で見ていきましょう。牛乳に栄養素が豊富なのは間違いないのですが、**栄養素が豊富な食品というのは消化が難しいことが多い**のです。よって、**消化不良が各種アレルギーや生活習慣病を引き起こす可能性**があります。消化能力は個人によって異なるので、消化能力が高い人には問題のない牛乳でも、消化能力が低い人には、牛乳を常飲することは問題を引き起こす可能性が高いのです。

　ただでさえ、**過食や栄養過多による肥満や生活習慣病が問題になる現代**なので、幼少期を除いては、いつまでも牛乳に頼らなくても、それ以外の乳製品であるチーズやヨーグルト、各種動物性たんぱく質で十分に栄養をとれているのかもしれません。いずれにせよ、どんな食品でも栄養が豊富だからと食べ続けるのではなく、***too much of a good thing*『過ぎたるは及ばざるがごとし』**を念頭に、適量の摂取にとどめておくのがよいのでしょう。

1 環境
2 社会
3 環境
4 健康
5 IT・テクノロジー
6 医学
7 環境
8 IT・テクノロジー
9 教育
10 社会

解答

問1 イ 　問2 ア 　問3 イ 　問4 ア 　問5 エ
問6 エ 　問7 ア、ウ

解説

問1

ア　農家や漁師は、今後やってくる数年で、自分たちが世界に十分な食料を供給できることを証明するだろう。

イ　今後、地球の気温が上昇することは、世界を飢餓に導く要因の1つになるかもしれない。

ウ　世界の人口は、21世紀半ばまでに、およそ17億人減るだろうと想定されている。

エ　食べるのに十分な食料を手にできない人は7億人しかいない。

　第1段落第5文 in the future, the biggest factor may be food shortages, due to ～, the impacts of global warming, ～. 「将来、(飢餓の)最大の要因は、～や、地球温暖化の影響、～による食料不足ということになるかもしれない」から、**イ**が正解。

　不正解の選択肢を見ていくと、アは、**第1段落第2文、第3文** Will the world's farms and fisheries be able to feed all those people? Probably not. 「世界の農場や漁場で、そのすべての人を養えるだろうか？　おそらく無理だろう」に反する。ウは、**第1段落第1文** The world's population is expected to **grow from around 7.3 billion today to more than 9 billion by 2050**, ～. 「世界人口は、2050年までには今日のおよそ73億人から90億人以上に増えると予想されていて～」に反する。エは、**第1段落第4文** Already, approximately **800 million people** in the world cannot get enough to eat. 「すでに、世界のおよそ8億人の人に、十分な食料が行き渡って

いない」に反する。

問2

　ア　異常なほどの大量の雨が降ったとしても、農業は将来影響を受け
　　　ないだろう。

　イ　農業は干ばつや洪水などの天気事象の影響を大きく受ける。

　ウ　農地の拡大は森林伐採を含むので、気候変動の原因となる。

　エ　気候変動のマイナスの影響も、確実に農業にダメージを与えるだ
　　　ろう。

　NOT問題（合わないものを選べ）なので、p.49の 解法 POINT ❷ で学ん
だように、消去法で解く。**第2段落第1文** Climate change is already
damaging agriculture in many countries, with longer and more
frequent droughts in some areas and flooding in others, and
the situation is bound to get worse. 「気候変動は、ある地域ではよ
り長くより頻繁な干ばつを伴い、また別の地域では洪水をもたらして、
すでに多くの国の農業にダメージを与えている。そして、**状況は悪くな
るばかりだ**」にアは反するので、正解。イ、エは同文に一致。ウは同段
落第2文に一致。

. . . .

問3

　ア　コーンのような作物から得た燃料を使う自動車は、資源を効率よ
　　　く使用している。

　イ　農地の面積が限られていることを考慮すると、私たちはそれを
　　　使って、燃料よりむしろ食料を生み出すべきだ。

　ウ　コーンは人間が消費する牛肉を生産するために栽培されるより
　　　も、車の燃料に使用されるべきだ。

　エ　人にではなく車に食べさせることは無駄でも非倫理的でもない。

　下線部の文構造から見ていく。

┌─ 構文図解 ─────────────────────────────

〈Feeding cars instead of people〉 is not only wasteful but also
　動名詞　　　　　　　　S　　　　　　　　V　　M　　　　C　　　not only A
　　　　　　　　　　　　　　　　　　　　　　　　　　　　　　　　but also B
very unethical.
　　　C

─────────────────────────────────────

Feedingが動名詞でpeopleまでの名詞のカタマリを作り、「人にではなく車に食べさせること」と、文のSを作る。**not only A but also B**は「**AだけではなくBも**」という**A**に**B**の情報が**追加**される表現。wasteful, very unethicalがCの第2文型の文。「**人にではなく車に食べさせることは、無駄であるだけではなく、大きく倫理に反する**」から、**車の燃料を作り出すことより、人間の食料を生み出すべきだ**となるので、**イ**が正解。**第3段落第1文 we will need to use our limited farmland much more efficiently.** から、イの **Considering the limited amount of farmland**の表現も問題ないことがわかる。

. . . .

問4

　ア　非常に多くの農地が、人間が消費する動物の飼育に使われているので、私たちの農地は無駄にされ続けている。

　イ　パームオイルを生産することは、車の動力に使われるとき、効率のよい農地の利用法だ。

　ウ　私たちは、牛のえさを作るのに使用される量を増やすような、農地のもっと効果的な管理を必要としている。

　エ　私たちは、農地が十二分にあるので、どう使うかを心配する必要がない。

　第3段落第2文 **One use of agricultural land that is particularly wasteful is for raising cattle or growing cattle feed.**「**農地の使用で特に無駄なものの1つに、牛の飼育や牛のえさの栽培がある**」から、**ア**が正解。ウは同文に反する。

　イ は 同 段 落 第5文 Another **wasteful use of farmland** is to produce corn, **palm oil,** and other crops for use as bio-ethanol in **car engines**.「農地のもう1つの**無駄な利用**は、**車のエンジン**のバイオエタノールとして利用するために、トウモロコシ、**パームオイル**、そして他の作物を作ることだ」に反する。

　エは**同段落第1文** 〜, we will need to use our limited farmland **much more efficiently.**「〜、私たちは、自分たちの限られた農地を**ずっと効率よく使う必要がある**」に反する。

. . . .

ア 国連食糧農業機関によると、世界で生産されている食料の一定量が廃棄されている。

イ 発展途上国での理想とは異なる方法で貯蔵、配達されている食料は、廃棄になる可能性がある。

ウ 販売者や顧客が果物を受け入れない1つの理由は、その質が悪いことが原因だ。

エ 廃棄物は、店主が消費期限を過ぎた食料を店で捨てることから生じるわけではない。

　問2に続いて**NOT問題**（合わないものを選べ）なので、消去法で解く。アは第4段落第1文に一致。**同段落第2文There are various reasons for this, such as inadequate storage and transportation facilities in developing countries,** the rejection by retailers or consumers of fruits and vegetables whose color, size or shape is below standard, **and the removal of food from stores when it passes its expiry date.**「これには、発展途上国の不適切な貯蔵や輸送施設、そして小売店や消費者が色、大きさ、形が規格外の果物を受け入れないこと、さらに消費期限を過ぎると、店で食料を廃棄するなどのさまざまな理由がある」にイ、ウは一致。エは反するので正解。thisは「世界中の食料の3分の1が廃棄されること」を指す。

論理 POINT ❻ there be 構文のSは抽象の目印

　there be構文のSは抽象表現の目印になるので、**その後に具体例がくると予測**できます。次の文の手前に「**例えば**」と補って、**見えない文のつながり**を見抜きます。

　第4段落第2文で、**There are various reasons for this**と**there be構文**が使われている。後ろの**such as**も具体例の目印になるが、**various reasons for this**「食料廃棄のさまざまな理由」が抽象表現で、その具体例として、

① inadequate storage and transportation facilities ～

② the rejection by retailers or consumers of fruits and vegetables ～

③ the removal of food from stores when it passes its expiry date

が挙げられている。本問ではイとウが一致するので不適、エが異なるので正解だとわかる。

・・

問6

ア　たとえもし日本人が動物性食品の消費を減らしても、これは食料危機に何も影響を与えないだろう。

イ　肉は、日本食の重要な一部ではまったくないと言うことができる。

ウ　日本の顧客は、より多くの肉を食べることで、もっと有益な貢献ができる可能性がある。

エ　日本人は肉を大量に食べるし、食べ残しの食料を大量に捨ててもいる。

　最終段落第1文 The amount of food thrown away in Japan could feed more than 30 million people each year.「毎年、日本で廃棄される食べ物の量で、3000万人以上を養うことができる」、同段落第2文 Japan is a significant consumer of meat「日本は、肉を大量に消費している」より、エが正解。イは同文に反する。アは同段落最終文に反する。ウは本文に記述なし。

・・

問7

ア　筆者は、今日では、貧困が飢饉の最も重要な要因とは考えていない。

イ　世界の気候変動の責任の一部は、農業の慣習にある。

ウ　気候変動の過程で、作物の増加だけが、温室効果ガスの要因として作用する。

エ　もし人間が牛肉を食べるのを控えるなら、世界の人々にもっと食料が行き渡るだろう。

オ　倫理的な観点から、人間に食料を供給することは、それを自動車の燃料として使用する前に、何よりも重要視すべきことだ。

カ　仮に日本人が食料を廃棄しなければ、さらに3000万人を超える人を養うことができる。

キ　日本人は、食品廃棄を減らし、肉の消費量を減らすことで、気候に与える影響を減らすことができるかもしれない。

問2、問5に続いて**NOT問題**（合わないものを選べ）なので、消去法で解く。アは**第1段落第5文**の the main cause of hunger now is poverty「**現在の飢餓の主な原因は貧困**」に反するので正解。アの **doubts that** に着目する。

>**語彙 POINT ⑤**　「疑う」の区別

　doubtは「**疑う**」という意味ですが、**suspect**と区別する必要があります。両方とも、目的語にthat節を伴うときが問題になりますが、**doubt that = don't think that**「**〜と思わない**」で、**suspect that = think that**「**〜と思う**」となることに注意しましょう。

>**語彙 POINT ⑤** の知識があれば、選択肢のアを正確に読み取って、正解に選ぶことができる。

　イは、**第2段落第2文**〜, agriculture is not just a victim of climate change, **it is also a major cause**, 〜「**農業は気候変動の犠牲者である**だけではない。それはまた、〜気候変動の**主な原因ともなっている。**」と一致するので、不正解。

　ウは、**第3段落第2文**に、農地の無駄な利用の1つが**牛の飼育や牛の餌を栽培すること**、**同段落第5文**に、農地のもう1つの無駄な利用が**車のエンジンに使用する作物の生産**とあり、農地の無駄な使用が気候変動に大きな影響を与えて温室効果ガスを増加させるので、**作物の増加だけが温室効果ガスの要因とは書かれておらず**、本文と反するので正解。

　エは、**第3段落第4文**に一致。オは、**第3段落最終文**に一致。カは、**最終段落第1文**に一致、キは、**最終段落最終文**に一致。

1 環境

2 社会

3 環境

4 健康

5 IT・テクノロジー

6 医学

7 環境

8 IT・テクノロジー

9 教育

10 社会

The world's population is expected to grow from around 7.3 billion
　　　　　　　S　　　　　　V　　　　to do
today to more than 9 billion by 2050, and is quite likely to reach 11
　　　　from A to B「AからBまで」　　　　　　　　　V　　　　　O
billion [by the end of the 21st century]. Will the world's farms and
　　　　　　　　　　M　　　　　　　　　　　　　　S
fisheries be able to feed all those people? Probably not. Already,
　　　　　V　　　　　　O　　　　　　　M　　　　　M
approximately 800 million people (in the world) cannot get enough
　　　S　　　　　　　　　　　　　　　　M　　　　　V　　　O
(to eat). [While the main cause of hunger now is poverty], [in the
　　　　　　「～だけれども」
不定詞 形容詞的用法　　　　　　　　　M　　　　　　　　　　　M
future], the biggest factor may be food shortages, [due to
　　　　　　S　　　　　　　V　　　C　　　　　　M
unsustainable farming practices, the impacts of global warming, and
unsustainable ~ practices, the impacts ~ warming, the relentless ~ populationの3つの接続
the relentless increase in the world's population].

Climate change is already damaging agriculture [in many
　　　S　　　　　　V　　　　　O　　　　M
countries], [with longer and more frequent droughts in some areas
　　　　　　　　　　　　　　M
and flooding in others], and the situation is bound to get worse.
droughts in ~ areasとflooding ~ othersの接続　S　　　V　　　C
However, agriculture is not just a victim (of climate change),
agricultureを指す M　　S　　V　　C　　　　　M
it is also a major cause, [responsible for significant greenhouse gas
S V　M　　　C　　　　being省略の分詞構文　　　M
emissions and for the clearing of forests to create more farmland].
　　for ~ emissionsとfor ~ farmlandの接続　不定詞 副詞的用法
[In order to feed more people later this century and to reduce the
　　　　　　M　　　　　to feed ~ centuryとto reduce ~ climateの接続
impact of agriculture on our climate], we will need to use our limited
　　　　　　　　　　　　　　　　　S　　　V　　　　　O
farmland much more efficiently.
　　　比較級の強調　　M

世界人口は、2050年までには今日のおよそ73億人から90億人以上に増えると予想されていて、21世紀末までには、110億人に達する可能性がかなり高い。世界の農場や漁場で、そのすべての人を養えるだろうか。おそらく無理だろう。すでに、世界のおよそ8億人の人に、十分な食料が行き渡っていない。現在の*飢餓の主な原因は貧困だが、将来、最大の要因は、持続性のない農業の慣習や、地球温暖化の影響、そして世界人口の絶え間ない増加による食料不足ということになるかもしれない。

気候変動は、ある地域ではより長くより頻繁な*干ばつを伴い、また別の地域では洪水をもたらして、すでに多くの国の農業にダメージを与えている。そして、状況は悪くなるばかりだ。しかし、農業は気候変動の犠牲者であるだけではない。それはまた、深刻な温室効果ガスの放出や、より多くの農地を作るために森林を伐採する原因になって、気候変動の主な要因ともなっている。

今世紀の後半に、より多くの人を養い、農業が私たちの気候に与える影響を減らすために、私たちは限られた農地をずっと効率よく使用する必要がある。

*「飢餓」は、食べ物がなくて飢えること。
*「干ばつ」は、長い間雨が降らず、農作物に必要な水が不足すること。

population	名	人口
around	前	およそ
billion	名	10億
be likely to do	熟	～しそうだ
fishery	名	漁場
feed	動	養う
approximately	副	およそ
hunger	名	飢餓
poverty	名	貧困
shortage	名	不足
due to	熟	～が原因で
unsustainable	形	持続性のない
impact	名	影響
global warming	名	地球温暖化

relentless	形	絶え間ない
agriculture	名	農業
frequent	形	頻繁な
drought	名	干ばつ
flooding	名	洪水
be bound to do	熟	きっと～する
victim	名	犠牲者
climate change	名	気候変動
responsible for	形	～の原因である
significant	形	深刻な
greenhouse gas	名	温室効果ガス
emission	名	放出
clearing	名	伐採
efficiently	副	効率よく

▶ 単語10回CHECK　1　2　3　4　5　6　7　8　9　10

1 環境
2 社会
3 環境
4 健康
5 IT・テクノロジー
6 医学
7 環境
8 IT・テクノロジー
9 教育
10 社会

One use (of agricultural land) (that is particularly wasteful) is [for
S　　　　　M　　　　　　　　　関係代名詞のthat　　　　M　　　　V　M

raising cattle or growing cattle feed]. [To produce 1 kilogram of beef
　　　raising cattle と growing ~ feed の接続　　不定詞 副詞的用法　　　　M

from grain-fed cattle], at least 7 kilograms (of grain) are needed. [If
　　　　　　　　　　　　　　S　　　　　M　　　　V　　M

we all gave up eating beef], a lot more people could be fed. Another
　　　　　　　　　　　　　　S　　　　V　　　　S

wasteful use (of farmland) is ⟨to produce corn, palm oil, and other
　　　　　　　M　　　　V　　不定詞 名詞的用法　　　　C

crops for use as bio-ethanol in car engines⟩. ⟨Feeding cars instead of
　　　　　　　　　　　　　　　　　　　　　　　動名詞　　　S

people⟩ is not only wasteful but also very unethical.
　　　V　　C　　　not only A but also B　　C

FAO research has shown ⟨that about one third of all food
S　　　　V　　　名詞節のthat　　　O

produced worldwide is eventually wasted⟩. There are various
過去分詞の名詞修飾　　　　　　　　　M　　V　　S

reasons (for this), ⟨such as inadequate storage and transportation
M　　世界中の食料の3分の1が廃棄されること　　　　M

facilities in developing countries, the rejection by retailers or

consumers of fruits and vegetables whose color, size or shape is below

standard, and the removal of food from stores when it passes its
　　　　　　　　　　　　　　　　　　foodを指す
　　　inadequate ~ countries, the rejection ~ standard, the removal ~ date の接続

expiry date⟩.

The amount (of food) (thrown away in Japan) could feed more
S　　　M　　過去分詞の名詞修飾　　M　　V　O

than 30 million people [each year]. Japan is a significant consumer
　　　　　　　　　　M　　　S　V　　　C

(of meat, mainly beef, pork, and chicken). Japanese consumers could
M　同格のカンマ　beef, pork, chicken の接続　　S　　V

make a contribution (to the looming food crisis and to reducing their
O　　　M　　to the looming ~ crisis と to reducing ~ climate の接続

impact on the world's climate) [by wasting less food and eating less
M　　　　　　　M　wasting less food と eating less meat の接続

meat].

本文訳

農地の使用で特に無駄なものの1つに、牛の飼育や牛のえさの栽培がある。穀物で育てる牛から1キロの牛肉を生み出すのに、少なくとも7キロの穀物が必要である。もし私たち全員が牛肉を食べるのをやめるなら、ずっと多くの人を養うことができる。農地のもう1つの無駄な利用は、車のエンジンの*バイオエタノールとして利用するために、トウモロコシ、*パームオイル、他の作物を作ることだ。人にではなく、車に食べさせることは、無駄なだけではなく、大きく倫理に反する。

　国連食糧農業機関の研究によると、世界中で生み出されるすべての食糧のおよそ3分の1が、最終的に無駄になるとわかっている。これには、発展途上国の不適切な貯蔵や輸送施設、そして色、大きさ、形が規格外の果物や野菜を、小売業者や消費者が拒絶すること、さらに消費期限を過ぎると、店で食料を廃棄するなどのさまざまな理由がある。

　毎年、日本で廃棄される食べ物の量で、3000万人以上を養うことができる。日本は、肉、主に牛肉、豚肉、鶏肉などを大量に消費している。日本の消費者は、食品廃棄を減らし、肉食を減らすことで、迫り来る食料危機や、世界の気候への影響を減らすことに貢献できる可能性がある。

* 「バイオエタノール」は、サトウキビやトウモロコシ、木材や古紙などのバイオマス（エネルギー）を発酵・蒸留させて作ったエタノールで、燃料として自動車に多く使用される。
* 「パームオイル」は、アブラヤシの果実から得られる植物油のこと。

語彙リスト

particularly	副 特に	transportation	名 輸送
wasteful	形 無駄な	facility	名 施設
raise	動 育てる	rejection	名 拒絶
cattle	名 （集合的に）牛	retailer	名 小売店
grain-fed	形 穀物で育てられた	standard	名 標準
give up	熟 やめる	removal	名 廃棄
crop	名 作物	expiry date	名 消費期限
instead of	熟 〜の代わりに	throw away	熟 捨てる
unethical	形 倫理に反する	contribution	名 貢献
eventually	副 最終的に	looming	形 迫り来る
storage	名 蓄え	crisis	名 危機

▶ 単語10回CHECK　1　2　3　4　5　6　7　8　9　10

95

The world's population is expected to grow from around 7.3 billion today to more than 9 billion by 2050, and is quite likely to reach 11 billion by the end of the 21st century. Will the world's farms and fisheries be able to feed all those people? Probably not. Already, approximately 800 million people in the world cannot get enough to eat. While the main cause of hunger now is poverty, in the future, the biggest factor may be food shortages, due to unsustainable farming practices, the impacts of global warming, and the relentless increase in the world's population.

Climate change is already damaging agriculture in many countries, with longer and more frequent droughts in some areas and flooding in others, and the situation is bound to get worse. However, agriculture is not just a victim of climate change, it is also a major cause, responsible for significant greenhouse gas emissions and for the clearing of forests to create more farmland.

In order to feed more people later this century and to reduce the impact of agriculture on our climate, we will need to use our limited farmland much more efficiently. One use of agricultural land that is particularly wasteful is for raising cattle or growing cattle feed. To produce 1 kilogram of beef from grain-fed cattle, at least 7 kilograms of grain are needed. If we all gave up eating beef, a lot more people could be fed. Another wasteful use of farmland is to produce corn, palm oil, and other crops for use as bio-ethanol in car engines. Feeding cars instead of people is not only wasteful but also very unethical.

FAO research has shown that about one third of all food produced worldwide is eventually wasted. There are various reasons for this, such as inadequate storage and transportation facilities in developing countries, the rejection by retailers or consumers of fruits and vegetables whose color, size or shape is below standard, and the removal of food from stores when it passes its expiry date.

The amount of food thrown away in Japan could feed more than 30 million people each year. Japan is a significant consumer of meat, mainly beef, pork, and chicken. Japanese consumers could make a contribution to the looming food crisis and to reducing their impact on the world's climate by wasting less food and eating less meat.

▶ 音読10回CHECK　1　2　3　4　5　6　7　8　9　10

1 環境
2 社会
3 環境
4 健康
5 IT・テクノロジー
6 医学
7 環境
8 IT・テクノロジー
9 教育
10 社会

背景知識が
広がるコラム

BACKGROUND KNOWLEDGE
Food loss

Food loss「フードロス（食品ロス）」とは、**売れ残り、食べ残し、期限切れ食品など、まだ食べることができる食品が廃棄されること**を言います。本文に登場したように、FAO（国連食糧農業機関）によると、世界規模では、**生産された食料の3割以上に及ぶおよそ13億トンが、毎年失われるか廃棄されている**ようです。これは世界の飢餓人口10億人を充分に養えるほどの量に相当すると指摘されています。

日本での *Food loss*は年600万トン以上と推測されています。日本での *Food loss*を防ぐ取り組みとして、**飲食店で食べ残した料理を持ち帰ることを促す取り組み**が全国で実施されています。環境省が命名した、飲食店で食べ残した料理の持ち帰りを促す取り組みであるmottECO（モッテコ）という活動があります。

続いて、**様々な事情で、品質に問題がないにもかかわらず市場で流通できなくなった食品を、生活困窮者などに配給する活動である *Food bank*（フードバンク）**があります。*Food loss*を減らして、食料を必要とする人に届ける活動です。日本語の「もったいない」という言葉と同様に、世界中で注目されている活動です。

そして、大量の *Food loss*を生み出してしまう日本の**3分の1ルール**も見直しが進んでいます。**3分の1ルール**とは、賞味期間の3分の1以内に小売店舗へ納品するという商慣習です。最初の3分の1の期間は卸売業者が小売店に納品する「**納品期限**」、次の3分の1の期間は小売店が商品を店頭に置く「**販売期限**」、最後の3分の1は消費者がその食品をおいしく食べられる期間の「**賞味期限**」で、これがフードロスを生み出す要因にもなっています。

この3分の1ルールを改善する取り組みが推進されています。また、カップ麺、袋麺や飲料なども、安全面を再検証した上で、**各メーカーが賞味期限を延長する動き**がみられます。

解答

A ア ② イ ①
B ② C ③ D ③ E ②、③、④

解説

A

（ア）

① 科学者 ② 感情 ③ シナリオ ④ コンピューター

空所（ア）を含む文は、The first step toward this is understanding what（ ア ）are.「これに向かう最初のステップは、（ ア ）とは何であるかを理解することだ」となる。**this**は、「テクノロジーに**感情知能**を持たせるようにすること」なので、② **emotions** が正解。

（イ）

① 例えば ② それゆえに ③ しかしながら ④ さらに

空所（イ）の前は、「プライバシーの問題はポール・エクマンを含む多くの人が心配していること」で、後ろは「私たちが通りを歩いていると、私たちが知らないうちに装置やスキャナーが顔の表情を記録する」と、**抽象⇒具体**の流れになっているので、① **For example** が正解。

1 環境

2 社会

3 環境

4 健康

5 ｜Ｔ・テクノロジー

6 医学

7 環境

8 ｜Ｔ・テクノロジー

9 教育

10 社会

B

① ポール・エクマンは、1980年代に感情を研究した数少ない科学者の一人だ。

② ポール・エクマンは、感情の研究から学ぶべきたくさんのことがあると考えていた。

③ ポール・エクマンは、私たちが感情を隠そうとするとき、顔の筋肉が少し動くことに気付いていなかった。

④ ポール・エクマンは、私たちが環境に害を与えるテクノロジーを使うのをやめるべきだと考えていた。

第3段落第2文 But American psychologist Paul Ekman saw a lot of potential in this field. 「しかし、アメリカの心理学者のポール・エクマンはこの分野にたくさんの可能性を見出した」とあり、this field は「感情という研究分野のこと」なので、② Paul Ekman thought there were a lot of things to learn from the study of emotion. が正解。①は本文に記述なし。③は、第3段落第5文に反する。④は本文に記述なし。

- -

C

解法 POINT ❺ 整序問題

整序問題のコツは、**動詞**を中心に組み立てることです。英語の品詞の中ではいちばん力が強く、その動詞の持っている型に文全体が左右されるからです。

本問では、② enable に着目する。**enable O to do**「Oが〜するのを可能にする」の型を取るので、**enable it to read people's moods** まで完成させる。空所の手前に**冠詞の the** があるので、名詞の app を続けて、残りの to は to enable 〜 として、**不定詞の副詞的用法**を使う。完成された英文は the {app to enable it to read people's moods} になる。4番目には it がくるので、③が正解。

- -

99

① 人間　② 感情　③ ペッパー　④ テクノロジー

　下線部(2)を含む文はit comforts someone when (2)it senses the person is sad「それは、その人が悲しいと感知すると、その人を慰める」から、**itは人間の感情を感知して慰められるもの**とわかる。前の文のS、さらに前の文のSをたどると、Pepperを指しているとわかるので、**③が正解**。

．．．

① 『her／世界でひとつの彼女』や『チャッピー』という映画の中で、人間はロボットのように動いたり感じたりしていた。

② 感情をさらに研究することで、私たちはテクノロジーに感情知能を持たせることができるかもしれない。

③ テクノロジーの会社は、さまざまな感情を正確に認識できるソフトウェアを現在作ろうとしている。

④ 浅川智恵子教授は、感情を感知するテクノロジーを利用するスマートフォンのアプリを開発している。

⑤ ペッパーは、人間が自分の周りの環境を認識できるように、浅川智恵子教授が発明した。

⑥ 日本でペッパーは2015年に発売されたが、今では顧客に食事を出すことができる。

⑦ 感情を感知するテクノロジーは、私たちが心配する必要がある問題を作り出してはいない。

⑧ 感情を感知するテクノロジーの恩恵の1つは、多くの人が私たちが知らないうちに顔の表情を記録できることだ。

解法 POINT ❻　5つ以上の選択肢の内容一致問題

　たいてい**大問の最後に置かれる5つ以上の選択肢がある内容一致問題**は、先読みのしようがないので、**段落を2つ読むごとに、処理できる選択肢がないかを見ていきます**。

　①はHer and Chappieをスキャニングすると、**第1段落第2文「人間のように考えたり感じたりできるロボット」**より、不適。

②は第1段落最終文 we may be getting close to making technology emotionally intelligent「私たちはテクノロジーに感情知能を持たせることに近付いているかもしれない」と、第2段落第1文 The first step toward this is understanding what emotions are.「これに向かう最初のステップは、感情とは何であるかを理解することだ」から正解とわかる。

③は、第3段落第6文 A number of technology companies have now started to use Dr. Ekman's work to create software 〜.「いくつかのテクノロジーの会社が、〜ソフトウェアを作るためにエクマン博士の研究を利用し始めた」、同段落第7文 By analyzing thousands of different faces, the software learns to recognize different emotions 〜.「数千の異なる顔を分析することで、そのソフトウェアが〜に異なる感情を認識するようになる」から正解。

④は第4段落最終文 Dr. Asakawa is working to refine the app to enable it to read people's moods.「浅川教授は、そのアプリを高度化して、人の心的状態を読み取ることを可能にする研究を続けている」に一致。

⑤は本文に記述なし。

⑥は第5段落第2文から、「日本で2015年に発売された」までは正しいが、「顧客に食事を出す」が書かれていないので不適。第5段落最終文では、あくまで「小売店で接客をしている」という表現にとどまっている。

⑦は最終段落第1文に反する。p.48の 論理 POINT ❸ で見たように、同文の some major challenges が抽象表現になる。次の文から具体例が続き、プライバシーの問題などを作り出すとあることから、不適。

⑧は最終段落第1文の some major challenges「いくつかの重大な課題」の具体例として挙げられている内容で、恩恵の1つとはならないので不適。

People have long imagined a world (where we interact with
　　　　S　　　　V　　　　　　　O　　　関係副詞　　　　　M
computers and robots as if they were normal human beings). Science
　　　　　　　　　　　　　　　　　　　　　　　　　　　　　　　　　　　S
　　　　　　　computers and robots を指す
fiction movies (such as Her and Chappie) show computers and robots
　　　　　　　　A such as B「BのようなA」　　　M　　　V　　　　O　　前置詞のlike
(that think and feel just like humans). [While scenarios like these
　関係代名詞のthat　　M　　　前置詞のlike　　　　M　　人間のように思考力や感情のあるロボット
exist only in the movies for now], we may be getting close [to making
　　　　　　　　　　　　　　　　　S　　　V　　　　C　　M　make O C
technology emotionally intelligent].

　　The first step (toward this) is 〈understanding what emotions
　　　S 感情とは何であるのかの分析　M　テクノロジーに感情知能を持たせること　　　C
are〉. It's a complicated area (of study). Scientists are often unable
　　　S V　　　　　O　　　　M　　M　　　　　S　　　　　　　V
to define emotions [in exact terms], [even though we generally
　　　O　　　　　　　M　　　　　名詞節のthatの省略　　　M
understand what people mean when they say they're sad or happy].
　　　　　　関係代名詞のwhat　　　　　　people を指す
[Back in the 1950s], few scientists studied emotion. But American
　　　M　　　　　　　S　　　　　V　　　O　　　　　　S
psychologist Paul Ekman saw (a lot of) potential [in this field]. He
　　　　　　　　　　　　　V　　M　　　O　　　M　感情の分析　S
began 〈analyzing facial expressions〉, and compiled a list (of over
　V　　　動名詞　　　O　　　　　　　V　　　O　　M
5,000 muscle movements). These muscle movements combine
　　　　　　　　　　　　　　　　　S　　　　　　V
[to form our different expressions]. His discovery (of micro
　不定詞　副詞的用法　結果「～して」　M　　　S　　M
expressions) ― facial expressions that last only a fraction of a second
　　　　　　　　　　M　　　　関係代名詞のthat
― allows us to read the emotions that people try to hide.
　　V　　O to do　　　　　　　関係代名詞のthat

　人間は、コンピューターやロボットと、通常の人間であるかのようにやり取りする世界を長い間、想像してきた。『her ／世界でひとつの彼女』や『チャッピー』のようなSF映画が、いかにも人間のように考えたり感じたりするコンピューターやロボットを映し出す。このようなシナリオは、今のところ映画の中でしか存在しないが、私たちはテクノロジーに感情知能を持たせることに近付いているかもしれない。

　これに向かう最初のステップは、感情とは何であるかを理解することだ。それは複雑な研究分野だ。たとえ私たちが一般的に人が悲しいとか幸せだとか言うとき、何を意味するのかを理解していても、科学者は、厳密な用語では感情を定義できないことが多い。

　1950年代に戻ると、感情を研究する科学者はほとんどいなかった。しかし、アメリカの心理学者のポール・エクマンは、この分野にたくさんの可能性を見出していた。彼は顔の表情を分析し始めて、5千以上の筋肉の動きのリストを編集した。こうした筋肉の動きが組み合わさって、私たちの様々な表情を形成する。微表情、すなわちほんの一瞬しか続かない表情を彼が発見したことで、私たちは人が隠そうとする感情を読み取ることができる。

☐ interact with	動 ～とやり取りする		☐ field	名 分野
☐ as if	接 まるで～かのように		☐ analyze	動 分析する
☐ scenario	名 シナリオ		☐ facial	形 顔の
☐ exist	動 存在する		☐ expression	名 表情
☐ get close to	熟 ～に近づく		☐ compile	動 編集する
☐ emotionally	副 感情的に		☐ muscle	名 筋肉
☐ intelligent	形 知的な		☐ combine	動 結合する
☐ complicated	形 複雑な		☐ form	動 形成する
☐ define	動 定義する		☐ discovery	名 発見
☐ exact	形 正確な		☐ micro	形 微小な
☐ term	名 用語		☐ last	動 続く
☐ generally	副 一般的に		☐ fraction	名 断片
☐ psychologist	名 心理学者		☐ hide	動 隠す
☐ potential	名 可能性			

▶ 単語10回CHECK　1 ☐　2 ☐　3 ☐　4 ☐　5 ☐　6 ☐　7 ☐　8 ☐　9 ☐　10 ☐

右欄: 1 環境　2 社会　3 環境　4 健康　5 IT・テクノロジー　6 医学　7 環境　8 IT・テクノロジー　9 教育　10 社会

(A number of) technology companies have now started ⟨to use
　　M　　　　　　　　S　　　　　　　V　　　　不定詞 名詞的用法 O
Dr. Ekman's work⟩ [to create software that recognizes human facial
　　　　　　　　　　不定詞 副詞的用法　　関係代名詞のthat　　　　M
expressions]. [By analyzing thousands of different faces], the
　　　　　　　　　　　　　　M　　　　　　　　　　　　　　　S
software learns to recognize different emotions [with greater and
　　　　　　　V　　　　　　　　O　　　　　　M　比較級 and 比較級
greater accuracy].　　　　　　　　　　　　　　　　　「ますます〜」

There are many possible uses (of emotion-sensing technology).
　　　M　V　　S　　　　　　　　　　　　M
Dr. Chieko Asakawa, a researcher at Carnegie Mellon University,
　　　S　　　　　同格のカンマ　　　　　　　S′
has been blind [since the age of 14]. She has been developing
　V　　C　　　　　M　　　　　　　S　　　　V
a smartphone app (that might be able to help people with
　　　O　　　　　関係代名詞のthat　　　　　M
disabilities). [Using the smartphone's camera and audio], the app
　　　　　　　分詞構文　　　　M　　　　　the appを指す　　　S
helps the user navigate their environment. It also recognizes people's
　V　　O　　do　　people を指す　　　S　M　　V　　O
faces and facial expressions [as they approach]. Dr. Asakawa is
　　　　　　　　　　　　　　時のas「〜すると」 M　　　S　　V
working [to refine the app to enable it to read people's moods].
　　　　不定詞 副詞的用法
　　　　障害者を助けることに加えてもう1つ M　　the appを指す
Another use (of emotion-sensing technology) can be illustrated
　S　　　　　　　　　M　　　　　　　　　V
[through human-shaped robots like Pepper]. [Launched in Japan in
　　　　M　　　　　　　前置詞のlike　　　分詞構文　M
2015], Pepper is an interactive companion robot. It's capable of
　　　S　V　　　　C　　　　　　　Pepperを指す S　V
recognizing basic human emotions and responding appropriately.
　　　　　　　　　O　　　　　　　　　V　　　M
　　　　　　　Pepperを指す
[For example], it comforts someone [when it senses the person is
　M　　　S　V　　O　　　　Pepperを指す　M
sad], or cracks a joke [when the person is feeling playful].
　　　　V　　O　　　　　　M

最近では、いくつかのテクノロジーの会社が、人間の顔の表情を認識するソフトウェアを作るために、エクマン博士の研究を利用し始めた。数千の異なる顔を分析することで、ソフトウェアがますます正確に異なる感情を認識するようになる。

　感情を感知するテクノロジーの利用法の可能性はたくさんある。カーネギーメロン大学の研究者である浅川智恵子教授は、14歳のころからずっと目が見えない。彼女は障害を持つ人の手助けができる可能性のあるスマートフォンのアプリの開発を続けている。スマートフォンのカメラと*オーディオを使うことで、そのアプリは、ユーザーがその環境をうまく進んで行く手助けをする。それはまた、人が近づくと、その顔や表情を認識する。浅川教授は、そのアプリを高度化して、人の心的状態を読み取ることを可能にする研究を続けている。

　感情を感知するテクノロジーのもう1つの利用法は、ペッパーのような人間の形をしたロボットで説明することができる。日本で2015年に発売されたペッパーは、双方向の対話型ロボットだ。それは基本的な人間の感情を認識して、適切に応答することができる。例えば、人が悲しんでいると感知すると、慰めるし、あるいは人が陽気な気分でいると、冗談を飛ばす。

*「オーディオ」は音響装置のこと。

語	品詞	意味	語	品詞	意味
a number of	熟	いくつかの	mood	名	心的状態
start to do	動	～し始める	illustrate	動	説明する
recognize	動	認識する	launch	動	発売する
learn to do	熟	～するようになる	interactive	形	双方向性の
with accuracy	熟	正確に	companion	名	仲間
blind	形	盲目の	be capable of	熟	～できる
app	名	アプリ	respond	動	応答する
disability	名	障害	appropriately	副	適切に
audio	名	オーディオ	comfort	動	慰める
help O do	動	Oが～するのを助ける	sense	動	感じる
navigate	動	進む	crack a joke	熟	冗談を言う
approach	動	近づく	playful	形	陽気な
refine	動	高度化する			

▶ 単語10回CHECK 　1　2　3　4　5　6　7　8　9　10

105

[In Japan], Pepper is already serving customers [in retail stores].
M　　　　S　　　　　V　　　　　　　O　　　　　　　M

[Although the idea of emotionally intelligent devices may sound
M
fascinating], this technology can create some major challenges. The
感情知能のある装置を作る技術　S　　　　V　　　O　　　　　　S
issue (of privacy) is something (that many people, including Paul
M　　　　V　　C　　　　関係代名詞のthat　　　　　M
Ekman, are concerned about). [For example], [as we walk on the
M　　　　　　　時のas　　　M
streets], devices and scanners could record our facial expressions
S　通りを歩いているときに、知らずに表情が記録されてしまうこと　V　　　　O
[without our knowledge]. This could allow many people to monitor or
M　　　　　　　S　　　V　　　　O　　　to do
view our feelings without permission. It may leave us no control
多くの人が許可なしに私たちの感情を監視して見ることができること　S　V　O₁　　O₂
(over who we share our feelings with). However, [if we can negotiate
疑問詞のwho「誰と〜か」　　　M　　　　M　　　　M
these challenges successfully], there could be many benefits [for all
知らずに表情を記録されたり、感情を監視されたりするなどの問題　M　V　　S　　　　M
of us] [if our devices become a little more human].
M

106

日本では、ペッパーはすでに小売店で接客をし始めている。

　感情知能付きの装置というアイデアは魅力的に聞こえるかもしれないが、このテクノロジーは、いくつかの重大な課題を引き起こす可能性がある。プライバシーの問題は、ポール・エクマンを含む多くの人が心配していることだ。例えば、私たちが通りを歩いていると、装置やスキャナーが、私たちが知らないうちに、顔の表情を記録できる。このために、多くの人が許可なしに私たちの感情を監視するか見ることができる可能性がある。それによって、私たちは自分の感情を誰と共有するかを、コントロールできなくなるかもしれない。しかし、もし私たちがこれらの課題をうまく乗り越えられるなら、もし身近にある装置がもう少し人間らしくなったなら、私たち全員に多くの恩恵があるかもしれない。

1	環境
2	社会
3	環境
4	健康
5	IT・テクノロジー
6	医学
7	環境
8	IT・テクノロジー
9	教育
10	社会

語 彙 リ ス ト

serve	動	仕える
customer	名	顧客
retail store	名	小売店
device	名	装置
sound	動	〜に聞こえる
fascinating	形	魅力的な
challenge	名	課題
issue	名	問題
privacy	名	プライバシー

be concerned about	熟	〜を心配している
scanner	名	スキャナー
record	動	記録する
monitor	動	監視する
permission	名	許可
negotiate	動	乗り越える
successfully	副	うまく
benefit	名	恩恵

▶ 単語10回CHECK　1　2　3　4　5　6　7　8　9　10

People have long imagined a world where we interact with computers and robots as if they were normal human beings. Science fiction movies such as Her and Chappie show computers and robots that think and feel just like humans. While scenarios like these exist only in the movies for now, we may be getting close to making technology emotionally intelligent.

The first step toward this is understanding what emotions are. It's a complicated area of study. Scientists are often unable to define emotions in exact terms, even though we generally understand what people mean when they say they're sad or happy.

Back in the 1950s, few scientists studied emotion. But American psychologist Paul Ekman saw a lot of potential in this field. He began analyzing facial expressions, and compiled a list of over 5,000 muscle movements. These muscle movements combine to form our different expressions. His discovery of micro expressions — facial expressions that last only a fraction of a second — allows us to read the emotions that people try to hide. A number of technology companies have now started to use Dr. Ekman's work to create software that recognizes human facial expressions. By analyzing thousands of different faces, the software learns to recognize different emotions with greater and greater accuracy.

There are many possible uses of emotion-sensing technology. Dr. Chieko Asakawa, a researcher at Carnegie Mellon University, has been blind since the age of 14. She has been developing a smartphone app that might be able to help people with disabilities. Using the smartphone's camera and audio, the app helps the user navigate their environment. It also recognizes people's faces and facial expressions as they approach. Dr. Asakawa is working to refine the app to enable it to read people's moods.

Another use of emotion-sensing technology can be illustrated through human-shaped robots like Pepper. Launched in Japan in 2015, Pepper is an interactive companion robot. It's capable of recognizing basic human emotions and responding appropriately. For example, it comforts someone when it senses the person is sad, or cracks a joke when the person is feeling playful. In Japan, Pepper is already serving customers in retail stores.

Although the idea of emotionally intelligent devices may sound fascinating, this technology can create some major challenges. The issue of privacy is something that many people, including Paul Ekman, are concerned about. For example, as we walk on the streets, devices and scanners could record our facial expressions without our knowledge. This could allow many people to monitor or view our feelings without permission. It may leave us no control over who we share our feelings with. However, if we can negotiate these challenges successfully, there could be many benefits for all of us if our devices become a little more human.

▶ 音読10回CHECK 〔1〕〔2〕〔3〕〔4〕〔5〕〔6〕〔7〕〔8〕〔9〕〔10〕

1 環境
2 社会
3 環境
4 健康
5 IT・テクノロジー
6 医学
7 環境
8 IT・テクノロジー
9 教育
10 社会

背景知識が広がるコラム

BACKGROUND KNOWLEDGE
Emotion AI

本文で登場した感情を読み取るソフトウェアとは、AIの一種で、***Emotion AI*（感情認識AI**）とも言われています。**感情認識AI**とは、**人間の感情を人工知能で読み取るシステム**のことです。様々な分野での活用の試みが行われています。

例えば、**自動車**において、ドライバーの眠気を感知した場合、AIが合成音声で眠気覚ましの提案を行う試みがあります。

教育分野では、**問題が難しすぎる**といった不満を顔の表情からとらえて、**AIが問題の難易度を調整する**試みが行われています。あるいは、**自閉症の児童の学習支援**として、ゲーム形式で、相手の感情を読み取る訓練を積むことができるものがあります。

その他、**顧客の感情を読み取ることで**、マーケティングへの活用が検討されたり、**医療分野では**、人間でも判断が難しいとされてきた**PTSD（心的外傷後ストレス障害）の発見に利用できる可能性**などが示唆されています。

設問1 実際に、1996年には、アメリカで世界初の「バーチャル大学」が設立されて、比較的短期間のうちに、遠隔学習がどれ程進歩したかを示した。

設問2 遠隔学習がいつでもどこでもできることがもたらす柔軟性は、学生が自分のペースでより上手に学習できることを意味するが、それはまた学習者がしっかりと準備をして、自己を律しなければならないことも意味する。

設問3 遠隔学習では、教師が学生とめったに会えないので、教師が学生の具体的な学習ニーズを理解することが難しくなるかもしれない。

設問4 対面学習でも遠隔学習でも、教師が知っている側なので、学生が講義の重要な部分を理解する手助けをする責任があり、教師が学習資料を提示する方法、話題を導入する順序を決めて、講義の課題を作ったり、どんな資料が学習に役立つかを学生に知らせて、何らかの方法で学生にフィードバックすること。

設問1

構文図解

Indeed, 1996 saw the establishment (of the world's first
M   S   V   O   主格のof「〜が」

"virtual university") [in the United States], [showing how far
      M   M   分詞構文「〜して、…」

distance learning has come in a relatively short space of time].
              M

この文のポイントは、① **時代の主語**、② **名詞構文**の2点あるので、順に解説する。

▌構文 POINT ❹▐ 時代の主語

（例文）
The 18th century saw the American Revolution.
訳 18世紀には、アメリカ独立戦争があった。
　「～世紀」、「～年」などの**時代や年代が主語**で、**動詞にsee**を使い、**目的語にそのときに起きた出来事**がくる表現があります。この場合、「その時代が～を目撃した」と訳すのではなくて、「**その時代に～があった**」と訳します。

　本問でも、**Sの1996をin 1996と読みかえて**、「**1996年に～**」と訳す。

▌構文 POINT ❺▐ 名詞構文

（例文）
She was moved by **the rise of the sun**.
訳 彼女は太陽が昇ってくる様子に感動した。
　名詞構文とは、和訳の技術の1つで、訳すときに**英語の名詞を日本語では動詞に読みかえる**と非常にきれいな訳出が可能になります。例文でも、**the rise of the sun**を「日の出」と訳してもよいのですが、ofを前後を**SV関係でつなぐ主格「～が」**ととらえて、riseを**V′**、the sunを**S′**として、「**太陽が昇ってくる様子**」とすると、きれいな日本語になります。

　本問でも、the establishment of the world's first "virtual university" は、establishmentを**V′**、ofを**主格「～が」**として、the ～ university" を**S′**とする。すると、「**世界初の『バーチャル大学』が設立された**」ときれいな日本語になる。showing以下は文尾の**分詞構文**なので、「**～して、…**」と訳出する。まとめると、「**実際に、1996年には、アメリカで世界初の『バーチャル大学』が設立されて、比較的短期間のうちに、遠隔教育がどの程度進歩したかを示した**」となる。

1 環境
2 社会
3 環境
4 健康
5 IT・テクノロジー
6 医学
7 環境
8 IT・テクノロジー
9 教育
10 社会

111

構文図解 　遠隔学習はいつでもどこでもできること

The flexibility (this provides) means 〈that students may be
S　　　　　関係代名詞の省略　　M　　　V　　名詞節のthat　　　　　O
better able to learn at their own pace〉, but it may also mean
　　　　　　　　　　　　　　　　　　　遠隔学習がもたらす柔軟性　　　V
〈that learners have to be well organized and self-disciplined〉.
　名詞節のthat　　　　　　　　　　　　　O

　The flexibility this provides が 名詞 SV の語順なので、**関係詞の省略**に気付く。this は前文の内容で、「**遠隔授業がいつでもどこでもできること**」を指す。The flexibility が S、means が V、that から名詞節が始まり、pace までの意味のカタマリを作って、文の O になる。but を挟んで、it は手前の「**遠隔学習がもたらす柔軟性**」を指す。

　続いて、**that から名詞節**が始まって、self-disciplined までの意味のカタマリを作り、「**学習者がしっかりと準備して自己を律しなければならないこと**」となる。まとめると、「遠隔授業がいつでもどこでもできることがもたらす柔軟性は、学生が自分のペースでより上手に学習できることを意味するが、それはまた学習者がしっかりと準備して自己を律しなければならないことも意味する」となる。

構文図解 　形式目的語のit

This may make it hard 〈for teachers to understand their
S　　　V　　O　C　不定詞のS　　不定詞 名詞的用法
students' specific learning needs〉.
　　　　　　　　　　O′

　This は基本的に前文を指すので、「バーチャル教室では教師と学生がめったに顔を合わせないこと」を指す。**make O C「O を C にする」**の第5文型で、**it が形式目的語で O、hard が C** になる。

　it は to 以下を指して、**to understand ～は不定詞の名詞的用法**。**for teachers は不定詞の主語**なので、「教師が～を理解すること」の意味になる。

1 環境

2 社会

3 環境

4 健康

5 IT・テクノロジー

6 医学

7 環境

8 IT・テクノロジー

9 教育

10 社会

構文 POINT ❻ 無生物主語＋make O Cは因果関係

無生物主語と**make O C**が合わさると、**主語とO Cの間に因果関係を作る**ことができます。**因果関係**は、設問と絡む可能性が非常に高いので、必ずチェックしましょう。

本問は、「このことが原因で、教師が学生の具体的な学習ニーズを理解するのが難しくなるかもしれない」で、「このこと」を具体化して、「**遠隔教育では、教師が学生にめったに会えないので、教師が学生の具体的な学習ニーズを理解するのが難しくなるかもしれない**」とする。

・・・

設問4

下線部(A)を含む文は、Although the nature of the teacher-student relationship may differ in the two methods, they do share the same (A)core principles.「教師と学生の関係性は、2つの方法で異なるかもしれないが、2つとも同じ核となる原則を実際には共有している」となる。p.48の 論理 POINT ❸ で学んだように、**複数名詞は抽象表現の目印**なので、以降の具体説明をまとめる。

「**2つの方法**」とは、**対面学習と遠隔学習**を指す。その後に「**教室では教師が『知っている側』であるように、教師は、学生がオンライン授業の重要な部分を理解する手助けをする責任者となる**」と、the same core principlesの説明が続く。以上をまとめると、「**対面学習でも遠隔学習でも、教師が知っている側なので、学生が講義の重要な部分を理解する手助けをする責任があり、教師が学習資料を提示する方法、話題を導入する順序を決めて、講義の課題を作ったり、どんな資料が学習に役立つかを学生に知らせて、何らかの方法で学生にフィードバックすること**」になる。

distance learningを指す

[Although many people think it is a modern phenomenon],
M　　　　　　　名詞節のthatの省略

distance learning has been around [for at least 200 years] [in one
S　　　　　V　　「存在している」　　　　M　　　　　　　　M

form or another]. Historical examples (of long-distance learning)
S　　　　　　　　　　　M

include ⟨students being sent a series of weekly lessons by mail⟩.
V　　　動名詞のS　動名詞　　　　　　　　　　O

The technological advances (of the past 20 or so years), however,
S　　　　　　　　　M　　　　　　　　　M

have meant ⟨that this form of education is now a credible alternative
V　　　名詞節のthat　　　　　　　　O

to face-to-face learning⟩. Indeed, 1996 saw the establishment (of the
M　　　S　V　　　　O　　　　主格のof

world's first "virtual university") [in the United States], [showing
M　　　　　　　　　M　　　　　分詞構文

how far distance learning has come in a relatively short space of
M

time]. [While it is now possible to obtain a large variety of online
形式主語　M　　不定詞 名詞的用法　　不定詞 形容詞的用法

degrees], which is the best type (of education) (to pursue)? A closer
S　V　　C　　　　M　　　　　M　　　S

examination (of this topic) reveals ⟨that distance and traditional
M　　　　V　名詞節のthat　　O

educational instruction have significant differences but also some

similarities⟩.

[When comparing the two systems], the most obvious difference
you（一般人を指す）areの省略　M　　　　　S

lies [in the way that instruction is delivered]. Distance learning is
V　　M　　the way that ~「~する方法」　　　S　　　V

heavily dependent on technology, particularly the Internet. [In a
O　　同格のカンマ　　O'　　　　M

face-to-face course], students may only require a computer [for the
S　　　V　　　　O　　　M

purpose of writing an essay]. [In comparison], [when learning
M　　　　　　　　M　　　you（一般人を指す）areの省略

remotely], technology is the principal means (of communication).
M　　　S　　V　　　C　　　　M

114

1 環境
2 社会
3 環境
4 健康
5 IT・テクノロジー
6 医学
7 環境
8 IT・テクノロジー
9 教育
10 社会

//////// 本 文 訳 ////////

　多くの人は現代の現象だと思うが、遠隔学習は、何らかの形で、少なくとも200年前から存在してきた。遠隔学習の過去の例には、郵便で毎週一連の授業の内容が学生に送られてくることなどがある。しかし、過去20年かそこらの技術的な進歩によって、この教育形態が、対面学習の信頼できる代替手段となっている。実際に、1996年には、アメリカで世界初の「*バーチャル大学」が設立されて、比較的短期間のうちに、遠隔学習がどの程度進歩したかを示した。現在ではオンラインで非常に多くの種類の学位を取ることが可能だが、どれが追求すべき最高の教育なのか。このテーマへのより綿密な調査によると、遠隔教育と従来からの教育には大きな違いはあるが、いくつかの類似点もあると明らかになっている。

　2つのシステムを比べると、最も明らかな違いは指導が届けられる方法にある。遠隔学習は、テクノロジー、とりわけインターネットに大きく依存している。対面授業では、学生は論文を書くためにコンピューターを必要とするだけであるかもしれない。それに対して、遠隔学習では、テクノロジーがコミュニケーションの主な手段になる。

*「バーチャル」とは、実体を伴わない仮想的な空間などを意味する。

//////// 語 彙 リ ス ト ////////

modern	形	現代の
phenomenon	名	現象
distance	名	距離
be around	熟	存在している
one ~ or another	熟	何らかの~
historical	形	歴史の
include	動	~を含んでいる
a series of	熟	一連の~
credible	形	信頼できる
alternative	名	代替手段
face-to-face	形	対面式の
indeed	副	実際には
establishment	名	設立
virtual	形	バーチャルの
relatively	副	比較的
a variety of	熟	様々な~
degree	名	学位

pursue	動	追求する
close	形	綿密な
examination	名	調査
topic	名	テーマ
reveal	動	明らかにする
instruction	名	指導
significant	形	重大な
similarity	名	類似点
lie	動	~にある
deliver	動	届ける
be dependent on	熟	~に依存している
heavily	副	大きく
particularly	副	特に
in comparison	熟	それに対して
principal	形	主要な
means	名	手段
communication	名	意思疎通

▶ 単語10回CHECK 　1　2　3　4　5　6　7　8　9　10

Face-to-face instruction must take place [in real time and in one
location]. Conversely, distance learning can happen [at any time and
in any location], [since the learning is not restricted by geography].
The flexibility (this provides) means ⟨that students may be better
able to learn at their own pace⟩, but it may also mean ⟨that learners
have to be well organized and self-disciplined⟩. [In other words],
they must be more highly motivated [in order to do well in distance-
learning courses]. Finally, [with face-to-face learning], the
teacher and student have the opportunity (to develop a personal
relationship). [In a virtual classroom], [by contrast], the teacher
may seldom or never actually meet the student. This may make
it hard ⟨for teachers to understand their students' specific learning
needs⟩.

[Although the nature of the teacher-student relationship may
differ in the two methods], they do share the same core principles.
[Just as a teacher is the "knower" in a classroom], he or she is the
one (responsible for helping students understand the key sections of
an online course). The teacher needs to decide ⟨how to best present
the material to be learned and in which sequence the topics should
be introduced⟩.

Annotations (構文図解):

- Face-to-face instruction = S / must take place = V / in real time and in one location = M
- distance learning = S / can happen = V / at any time and in any location = M / 理由の since「〜ので」
- since the learning is not restricted by geography = M
- 遠隔学習はいつでもどこでもできること
- The flexibility = S / 関係代名詞の省略 / this provides = M / means = V / 名詞節の that / that students may be better able to learn at their own pace = O
- 遠隔学習がもたらす柔軟性 S / it = S / may also mean = V / 名詞節の that / that learners... = O
- learners を指す / they = S / must be = V / more highly motivated = C / in order to do well in distance-learning courses = M
- with face-to-face learning = M / the teacher and student = S / have = V / the opportunity = O
- 不定詞 形容詞的用法 / to develop a personal relationship = M
- In a virtual classroom = M / by contrast = M / the teacher = S
- 教師が生徒にめったに会わないこと
- may = V / seldom or never actually meet = V / the student = O / This = S / may make = V
- 形式目的語の it / it = O / hard = C / for teachers = 不定詞の S / to understand = 不定詞 名詞的用法 / their students' specific learning needs = O'
- Although the nature of the teacher-student relationship may differ in the two methods = M
- the two methods を指す / they = S / 強調の助動詞 do「実際に」/ do share = V / the same core principles = O
- Just as a teacher is the "knower" in a classroom / 様態の as「ちょうど〜のように」/ M / he or she = S / is = V / the one = C
- 形容詞の後置修飾 / responsible for helping students understand the key sections of an online course / help O do の do / M
- The teacher = S / needs to decide = V / how to do「〜する方法」/ how to best present the material to be learned and in which sequence the topics should be introduced = O
- 不定詞 形容詞的用法 / どういった順番で〜か

1	環境
2	社会
3	環境
4	健康
5	IT・テクノロジー
6	医学
7	環境
8	IT・テクノロジー
9	教育
10	社会

本 文 訳

対面授業は、リアルタイムで1つの場所で行われなければならない。逆に、遠隔学習は、地理的な制約に縛られていないので、いつでもどこでも行うことが可能だ。これがもたらす柔軟性は、学生が自分のペースでより上手に学習できることを意味するが、それはまた学習者はしっかりと準備して自己を律する必要があることも意味する。すなわち、学習者は遠隔授業でしっかりと学ぶために、より高いモチベーションを持たなければならない。最後に、対面学習には、教師と学生が個人的な関係を築く機会がある。対照的に、バーチャルな教室では、教師が実際に学生に会うことはめったに、あるいはまったくないかもしれない。このせいで、教師が学生の具体的な学習ニーズを理解することが難しくなるかもしれない。

　教師と学生の関係性は、2つの方法で異なるかもしれないが、2つとも同じ核となる原則を実際には共有している。教室では教師が「知っている側」であるように、教師は、学生がオンライン授業の重要な部分を理解する手助けをする責任者となる。教師は学習資料を最善な形で提示する方法、そしてどういった順番でその話題を導入すべきかを決定する必要がある。

語 彙 リ ス ト

take place	熟	起こる		opportunity	名	機会	
location	名	場所		relationship	名	関係	
conversely	副	逆に		by contrast	熟	対照的に	
at any time	熟	いつでも		seldom	副	めったに〜ない	
restrict	動	制限する		specific	形	具体的な	
geography	名	地理		differ	動	異なる	
flexibility	名	柔軟さ		method	名	方法	
provide	動	供給する		core	形	核となる	
organize	動	準備する		principle	名	原則	
self-disciplined	形	自己を律する		responsible for	熟	〜に責任のある	
in other words	熟	すなわち		section	名	部分	
highly	副	非常に		present	動	提示する	
motivate	動	動機づける		material	名	資料	
in order to do	熟	〜するために		sequence	名	順番	
course	名	授業		introduce	動	導入する	

▶ 単語10回CHECK　1　2　3　4　5　6　7　8　9　10

He or she must also create the assignments (for the course) and help
　　　S　　　　　　　　V　　　　　　　　　O　　　　　　　　　M　　　　　V

the students know what resources (textbooks, websites, and so on)
　　O　　　do
　　　　　　　　　　疑問形容詞の what「どの名詞が〜か」

will best support their learning. Additionally, a teacher needs to
　　　　　　　　　　　　　　　　　　　　　　M　　　　　　S　　　　V

provide student feedback [in some way]. [For example], a language
　　　　　O₁　　　　O₂　　　　M　　　　　　　M　　　　　　S

teacher (in a classroom) may be able to correct a student's grammar
　　　　　　M　　　　　　　　V　　　　　　　　　　O

or pronunciation [in the moment], [whereas a distance-learning
　　　　M　　　　　　　　　　　　　　　「一方で」　　　　M

teacher may need to provide written or recorded feedback to be
　　　　　　　　　　　　　　　　　　　　　　　　　　　　　　不定詞 形容詞的用法

delivered later]. [In any case], all the usual elements (of the
　　　　　　　　　　　M　　　　　　　S　　　　　　　M

teacher's role) are necessary, [no matter what kind of instruction is
　　　　　　　　V　　　C　　　　　　　　　　　　M

being used].

本 文 訳

教師は授業の課題を作ったり、学生がどんな資料（テキスト、ウェブサイトなど）が自分の学習に最も役に立つかを知る手助けもしなければいけない。さらに、教師は何らかの方法で生徒に*フィードバックをする必要がある。例えば、語学の教師は教室で、その場で学生の文法や発音を直せるかもしれない。その一方で、遠隔学習の教師は、のちに紙か録音された*フィードバックを届ける必要があるかもしれない。いずれにせよ、たとえどの種類の指導が行われていようが、教師の役割のあらゆる通常の要素は必要なものとなる。

* 「フィードバック」とは、サービスの利用者からの意見などを関係者へ伝えることを意味する。本問では、遠隔学習の教師が学生に伝える意見や評価を指す。

右側の章インデックス:

1 環境
2 社会
3 環境
4 健康
5 IT・テクノロジー
6 医学
7 環境
8 IT・テクノロジー
9 教育
10 社会

語 彙 リ ス ト

英語	品詞	意味
assignment	名	課題
resource	名	資料
and so on	熟	～など
support	動	支える
additionally	副	さらに
feedback	名	フィードバック
correct	動	訂正する
grammar	名	文法

英語	品詞	意味
pronunciation	名	発音
moment	名	瞬間
whereas	接	一方で
in any case	熟	いずれにせよ
usual	形	通常の
element	名	要素
role	名	役割
no matter 疑問詞	熟	たとえ～でも

▶ 単語10回CHECK 1 2 3 4 5 6 7 8 9 10

119

Although many people think it is a modern phenomenon, distance learning has been around for at least 200 years in one form or another. Historical examples of long-distance learning include students being sent a series of weekly lessons by mail. The technological advances of the past 20 or so years, however, have meant that this form of education is now a credible alternative to face-to-face learning. Indeed, 1996 saw the establishment of the world's first "virtual university" in the United States, showing how far distance learning has come in a relatively short space of time. While it is now possible to obtain a large variety of online degrees, which is the best type of education to pursue? A closer examination of this topic reveals that distance and traditional educational instruction have significant differences but also some similarities.

When comparing the two systems, the most obvious difference lies in the way that instruction is delivered. Distance learning is heavily dependent on technology, particularly the Internet. In a face-to-face course, students may only require a computer for the purpose of writing an essay. In comparison, when learning remotely, technology is the principal means of communication. Face-to-face instruction must take place in real time and in one location. Conversely, distance learning can happen at any time and in any location, since the learning is not restricted by geography. The flexibility this provides means that students may be better able to learn at their own pace, but it may also mean that learners have to be well organized and self-disciplined. In other words, they must be more highly motivated in order to do well in distance-learning courses. Finally, with face-to-face learning, the teacher and student have the opportunity to develop a personal relationship. In a virtual classroom, by contrast, the teacher may seldom or never actually meet the student. This may make it hard for teachers to understand their students' specific learning needs.

Although the nature of the teacher-student relationship may differ in the two methods, they do share the same core principles. Just as a teacher is the "knower" in a classroom, he or she is the one responsible for helping students understand the key sections of an online course. The teacher needs to decide how to best present the material to be learned and in which sequence the topics should be introduced. He or she must also create the assignments for the course and help the students know what resources (textbooks, websites, and so on) will best support their learning. Additionally, a teacher needs to provide student feedback in some way. For example, a language teacher in a classroom may be able to correct a student's grammar or pronunciation in the moment, whereas a distance-learning teacher may need to provide written or recorded feedback to be delivered later. In any case, all the usual elements of the teacher's role are necessary, no matter what kind of instruction is being used.

▶ 音読10回CHECK　1　2　3　4　5　6　7　8　9　10

1 環境
2 社会
3 環境
4 健康
5 IT・テクノロジー
6 医学
7 環境
8 IT・テクノロジー
9 教育
10 社会

背景知識が広がるコラム

BACKGROUND KNOWLEDGE
映像授業

　映像授業を初めて予備校で担当してから、優に10年を超える歳月が過ぎました。気付いたら、生徒が目の前にいて授業を行う対面授業より長い時間を、映像授業に費やしてきたことになります。初めて映像授業の収録に臨んだときの冷や汗のようなものは、いまだにはっきり覚えています。一度やられた方は、映像授業の大変さに気付いて、二度と軽口をたたかないようになるものだと思います。

　幸いなことに、まだまだ経験の浅い時期から映像授業に抜擢(ばってき)していただき、今まで必死にやってきました。**これでよいものかと常に自問自答の日々でしたが、何とか10年以上続けてこられて、多くの生徒が、私の映像授業で英語の成績が上がり、大学に受かり、人生が変わったと言ってくれている**ので、それなりの存在意義はあるのかと受け止めています。

　映像授業の手ごたえなんて数えるほどしか経験したことはありませんが、それでも、**制約の中で最善を尽くす**、映像授業とは、まさにそんな世界です。カメラに向かって、独り語りをするだけなので、決して楽しいようなものではありません。それでも、私の映像授業によって、経済的、地理的要因で授業を受けられなかった人に教育を届けられることに、少しずつ手ごたえを感じている昨今です。

解答

問1 ④   問2 ④   問3 ①   問4 ③   問5 ①

解説

問1

① 新しいライフスタイルは、在宅勤務だと実践できない。
② 在宅勤務のおかげで、労働者はインターネットを使って家族とコミュニケーションをとることができる。
③ 在宅勤務は、柔軟な労働時間を可能にして、オフィス内のやりとりを促す。
④ 交通機関が混み合う時間を避けられることは、在宅勤務者にとっての1つの恩恵である。

　第1段落第6文 Telecommuting eliminates the rush hour commute for workers「在宅勤務は、従業員のラッシュアワーの通勤をなくす」から、④ Avoiding busy traffic times is one benefit for telecommuting employees. が正解。本文の eliminates the rush hour commute が、選択肢の Avoiding busy traffic times にパラフレーズされていることに注意する。

　不正解の選択肢を見ていくと、第1段落第3文 This recent trend is called "telecommuting" or "teleworking."「この最近の傾向は、"在宅勤務"とか"テレワーク"と呼ばれる」より、新しいライフスタイルとは、在宅勤務を指すので、①は不適。②、③は本文に記述なし。

1	環境
2	社会
3	環境
4	健康
5	ＩＴ・テクノロジー
6	医学
7	環境
8	ＩＴ・テクノロジー
9	教育
10	社会

問2

① テクノロジーのおかげで、労働者は仕事ができる場所をより柔軟に決めることができる。
② 職場の雰囲気は、そこで何十年も働く人にとっては重要だ。
③ 個人デスクを持たないことは生産的だとわかっている。
④ ホットデスキングやオフィシングのおかげで、従業員は家で仕事ができる。

本問は**NOT問題**と同じなので、消去法で本文と矛盾する選択肢を探す。**第2段落第4文** 〜 "hotdesking" is a system where workers do not have assigned desks.、**同段落第5文** They come into the office and sit at a group of desks on a first-come, first-served basis. から、「ホットデスキング」とは、個人デスクを置かずに、出社した順に空いているデスクに座るシステムとわかる。従業員が家で仕事をするシステムではないので④が正解。

①は第2段落第1文 the technology supports a more mobile working style「テクノロジーがより流動的な働き方を支援する」に一致。②は**同段落第2文** However, workers spend about 40 years of their lives in jobs, so the work environment is an important concern.「しかしながら、労働者は人生のおよそ40年を仕事に費やすので、労働環境は重大な関心事だ」に一致。

③は**同段落最終文** These also have proven to be **efficient** for workers「これら（オープンシーティング、ホットデスキングなど）は労働者にとって**効率的**だ」に一致。

問3

第3段落最終文 "Co-working" can help solve feelings of isolation and loneliness for some telecommuters.「『コワーキング』は、一部の在宅勤務者にとって、孤立感や孤独感を解消する助けとなる可能性がある」から、①が正解。「コワーキング」とは、知らない者同士が共有スペースで働くことを指す。「ホテリング」とは、短時間オフィスを使う人が利用するシステムのことで、必要なときにオフィスのデスクを予約するもの。実際のホテルとは関係ないので、②、④は不適。③は本文に記述なし。

① 新しい働き方は、上司により多くのストレスを作り出す。
② 従来のオフィスのテクノロジーのおかげで、従業員は快適になる。
③ オフィスでの対人コミュニケーション、そしてビジネスのコミュニケーションは、簡単には置き換えられない。
④ 高い緊張感や孤独感を感じたりする人は、家で働くことができる。

最終段落第5文 The traditional office is not only a business environment but also an important social environment. 「従来のオフィスは、仕事上の環境であるだけでなく、人と交わる重要な環境だ」から、③が正解。

不正解の選択肢を見ていくと、①は、**同段落第2文** Some workers may try too hard to meet their employer's expectations. 「雇用者の期待に応えようとがんばりすぎる従業員がいるかもしれない」、同段落第3文 This could **result in** increased stress and overwork. 「このせいで、ストレス過多や過労につながる可能性がある」に反するので、不適。

論理 POINT 7 result in は因果関係の目印

　最終段落第3文の**result in**は直訳では「〜という結果になる」ですが、**主語と目的語に因果関係を作り出す**ので、主語から目的語に矢印を引きます。因果関係は、本問のように、設問になる可能性が高いので、要注意です。**主語から目的語に因果関係の矢印を引ける表現**に、以下のようなものがあります。
cause ／ lead to ／ bring about ／ result in
be responsible for

②は、**最終段落第6文** Some workers feel more comfortable socially in a traditional office. 「労働者の中には、従来のオフィスで仕事をすることを、人付き合いのうえでより快適に感じる人もいる」から、**一部の従業員はそう感じるが、すべての従業員がそう感じるわけではない**ので、不適。

④は、**最終段落第4文** Meeting new business contacts is more limited, and some workers feel more isolated. 「新しい仕事の関係者と会うことがより限られていて、もっと孤独を感じる労働者もいる」

から、新しい働き方（**在宅勤務など**）で**孤独感を覚える人がいる**という内容なので、不適。

問5

① ワークスペースの共有やオフィスの座席の配置の変更は、効果的になる可能性がある。
② ラウンジをシェアすることは、ホットデスキングとホテリングの成功にとても重要だ。
③ 従来のオフィスは、社交上の環境としては機能しない。
④ 従業員の孤立やストレスの問題は、在宅勤務で解決できるかもしれない。

　第2段落最終文 These also have proven to be efficient for workers and financially rewarding for companies. 「こうしたものは、労働者にとって効率的で、企業には財政面でプラスになることもわかっている」に着目する。p.27の ▎**論理 POINT ❷** より、these（＋ **名詞**）は、前の表現を抽象化したものなので、These はホットデスキングや座席の配置を変更できるモバイルデスクやオフィシングを指すとわかる。**第3段落最終文**でも、コワーキング、すなわちオフィスの共有は孤独感の解消につながるとあるので、①が正解。

　②は、ラウンジの話は**第3段落第5文、第6文**に登場するが、**ラウンジをシェアするのはコワーキングについてのことで、ホットデスキングやホテリングとの関連は説明されていない**ので、不適。

　③は**最終段落第5文** The traditional office is not only a business environment but also **an important social environment.** 「**従来のオフィスは、仕事上の環境であるだけでなく、人と交わる重要な環境でもある**」に反する。

　④は最終段落第3文、第4文 This could result in **increased stress and overwork.** ～ and some workers **feel more isolated.** にあるとおり、**在宅勤務が孤立やストレスにつながる可能性がある**、という内容に反するので不適。

Recently, alternative work styles are giving workers the
 M   S   V   O₁   O₂
opportunity ⟨to work in totally different environments⟩. Imagine
              不定詞 形容詞的用法   M   V
⟨making a cup of coffee in your kitchen⟩ and ⟨starting to work by
 動名詞   O   making ~ kitchen と starting ~ home の接続   O
turning on your computer in your office at home⟩. This recent trend
                                               新しい働き方   S
is called "telecommuting" or "teleworking." Some companies have
 V   C   S   V
closed their offices and all ⟨of their employees and managers⟩ are
                 O   S   M   V
telecommuting. Other companies have assigned certain employees
                        S   V   O
to work in this way. Telecommuting eliminates the rush hour
 to do   在宅勤務のこと   S   V   O
commute [for workers] and saves companies thousands of dollars [in
 M   V   O₁   O₂
rent and utilities for office space]. Will more companies consider
         M   S   V
⟨working at home⟩ or other alternative work styles? Does this mean
 動名詞   O   O   多くの会社が在宅勤務や新しい働き方を想定すること S   V
⟨that the traditional work style will fade away in the future⟩?
 名詞節の that   O
⟨A number of⟩ companies are using a combination ⟨of traditional and
 M   S   V   O   M
alternative work styles⟩. Many workers and companies are looking
                                 S   V
for more flexibility [to help make their work and personal lives more
 O   不定詞 副詞的用法   M   名詞節の that
convenient, efficient and productive]. Some companies claim ⟨that
         convenient, efficient, productive の接続   S   V   O
alternative work styles lead to higher productivity⟩. These new
                                在宅勤務などの新しい働き方   S
working styles are already being practiced [in many technology
         V   M
companies].

1 環境

2 社会

3 環境

4 健康

5 IT・テクノロジー

6 医学

7 環境

8 IT・テクノロジー

9 教育

10 社会

本文訳

　最近、新しい働き方が、労働者にまったく違った環境で働く機会を提供している。台所で一杯のコーヒーを作って、自宅のオフィスでコンピューターに電源を入れて働き始めることを想像してみよう。この最近の傾向は、「在宅勤務」とか「テレワーク」と呼ばれる。オフィスを閉めて、従業員や経営者の全員が在宅勤務をしている会社もある。また、一定数の従業員にこうした働き方を割り当てている会社もある。在宅勤務は、従業員のラッシュアワーの通勤をなくして、会社はオフィスの数千ドルもの賃貸料や公共料金を節約できる。より多くの会社が在宅勤務やほかの新しい働き方を考えるだろうか。このことは、従来の働き方が将来消えていくことを意味するのか。会社の中には、従来の働き方と新しい働き方を組み合わせているところもある。多くの労働者や企業が、自分たちの仕事やプライベートをより便利に、効率よく生産的にするのを助けるために、さらなる柔軟性を模索している。新しい働き方が、より高い生産性を生み出すと主張する会社もある。こうした新しい働き方は、多くのテクノロジーの会社ですでに実践されている。

語彙リスト

alternative	形 新しい	thousands of	熟 何千もの〜
opportunity	名 機会	rent	名 賃貸料
totally	副 まったく	utility	名 公共料金（電気・ガス・水道など）
environment	名 環境		
turn on	熟 電源を入れる	traditional	形 従来の
trend	名 傾向	fade away	熟 消え失せる
telecommuting	名 在宅勤務	combination	名 組み合わせたもの
employee	名 従業員	flexibility	名 柔軟性
manager	名 経営者	convenient	形 便利な
assign O to do	動 Oに〜することを割り当てる	efficient	形 効率のよい
certain	形 一定の	productive	形 生産的な
eliminate	動 削除する	claim	動 主張する
commute	名 通勤	lead to	動 〜を引き起こす
save O_1 O_2	動 O_1のO_2を節約する	practice	動 実践する

▶ 単語10回CHECK　1　2　3　4　5　6　7　8　9　10

Alternative work styles are increasing [in popularity] [because
　　　　　　　S　　　　　　　　V　　　　　　　　　M　　　　　M

the technology supports a more mobile working style]. However,
　　　　　　　　　　　　　　　　　　　　　　　　　　　　　　　　　　M

workers spend about 40 years (of their lives) [in jobs], so the work
　　S　　　V　　　　　O　　　　　　　　M　　　　　M　　　　　　　S

environment is an important concern. This trend has created other
　　　　　　V　　C　テクノロジーが流動的な働き方を可能にする傾向 S　　　　V　　　　O

alternative working styles (including "open seating" or "hotdesking,"
　　　　　　　　　　　　　　　　「～を含んで」　　　　　　　　M

"officing," "hoteling," and "co-working)." "Open seating" or
open seating or hotdesking, officing, hoteling, co-workingの接続　　　S

"hotdesking" is a system (where workers do not have assigned
　　　　　　　V　　C　　関係副詞　　　　　　　M

desks). They come [into the office] and sit [at a group of desks] [on a
workersを指す S　V　　　M　　　　　　V　　　　M　　　　　M

first-come, first-served basis]. Another similar concept is mobile
　　　　　　open seating, hotdeskingに加えてもう1つ　　　S　　　V　　C

desks or "officing." Mobile desks can be moved [into different
同格のor「すなわち」　　　S　　　　V　　　　M

arrangements] [for individual work or teamwork]. These also have
　　M　　　open seating, hotdesking, officing　S　　M　　V

proven to be efficient [for workers] and financially rewarding [for
　　　　　　　C　　　　　M　　　　　　　　M　　　　C　　　M

companies].

Moreover, alternative work styles can also include ⟨relocating to
　M　　　　S　　　　　　　　V　　　O　動名詞

other work spaces⟩. "Hoteling"can be used [for consultants or other
　　　　　　　　　　　S　　　V　　　　M

freelance groups that only need office space for a short period].
　　　　　　関係代名詞のthat

Seating (at desks in the office) is arranged [by the company] [only
　S　　　　M　　　　　　V　　　　　M

when needed].
　M　　it (seating) isの省略

1 環境

2 社会

3 環境

4 健康

5 IT・テクノロジー

6 医学

7 環境

8 IT・テクノロジー

9 教育

10 社会

本 文 訳

　新しい働き方がますます人気になっているのは、テクノロジーがより流動的な働き方を可能にするからだ。しかしながら、労働者は人生のおよそ40年を仕事に費やすので、労働環境は重大な関心事だ。この傾向は、「オープンシーティングやホットデスキング」、「オフィシング」、「ホテリング」、「コワーキング」などの他の新しい働き方を作ってきた。「オープンシーティング」や「ホットデスキング」は、労働者が個人のデスクを持たないシステムだ。労働者たちはオフィスにやってきて、早い者順にデスクに座る。もう1つの似たような概念は、モバイルデスク、すなわち「オフィシング」だ。モバイルデスクは、個人の仕事やチームの作業に応じて、さまざまに配置できる。こうしたものは、労働者にとって効率的で、企業には財政面でプラスになることもわかっている。

　さらに、新しい働き方には、他のワークスペースに移転することも含まれる。「ホテリング」は、短時間しかオフィスを必要としないコンサルタントや他のフリーランスの集団に使用されるものだ。オフィスのデスクの座席は、必要な時にだけ会社が配置する。

語 彙 リ ス ト

popularity	名 人気	prove to be C	動 Cとわかる
mobile	形 流動的な	financially	副 金銭的に
concern	名 懸念事項	rewarding	形 価値のある
on a ~ basis	熟 ~の基準で	moreover	副 さらに
a first-come, first-served	形 早い者勝ちの	relocate	動 移転する
concept	名 概念	period	名 期間
arrangement	名 配置	arrange	動 配置する
individual	形 個々の		

▶ 単語10回CHECK ⬜1 ⬜ ⬜2 ⬜ ⬜3 ⬜ ⬜4 ⬜ ⬜5 ⬜ ⬜6 ⬜ ⬜7 ⬜ ⬜8 ⬜ ⬜9 ⬜ ⬜10 ⬜

"Co-working" is a very different alternative work style. Co-working
　　S　　　V　　　　　　　　　　　　C　　　　　　　　　　　　S
spaces (in apartment buildings) combine the informal atmosphere
　　　　　　　　M　　　　　　　　　V　　　　　　　　O
(of the home office) [with a relaxed coffee lounge environment]. Co-
　　　　M　　　　　　　　combine A with B「AをBと結び付ける」　　M　　S
workers rent a private desk (in the apartment) and share the
　　　　V　　　O　　　　　　　　M　　　　　　　　V　　O
common areas, which may include meeting areas, office equipment
　　　　　　　「(そして)それは」　V　　　　　　　　O
and lounge space. "Co-working" can help solve feelings (of
meeting areas, office equipment, lounge spaceの3つの接続　S　　V　　help do　　O
isolation and loneliness) [for some telecommuters].
　　　　M　　　　　　　　　M

On the other hand, 〈working at home or in other alternative work
　　　　M　　　　　動名詞　　　　　　　　　　　　S
styles〉 is not always the perfect solution. Some workers may try [too
　　　V　　M　　　　　　C　　　　　　　　　S　　　　V　　M
hard] [to meet their employer's expectations]. This could result in
不定詞 副詞的用法　　　　O　　　　　　　　　S　　　V
increased stress and overwork. 〈Meeting new business contacts〉 is
　　　　　O　　　　　　　　　動名詞　　　　S　　　V
more limited, and some workers feel more isolated. The traditional
　C　　　　　S　　　　V　　　C　　　　　S
office is not only a business environment but also an important social
　V　　　　　　C　　　　　　　not only A but also B　　C
environment. Some workers feel more comfortable socially [in a
　　　　　　　S　　　V　　　C　　　　M　　M
traditional office]. Hopefully, more research will help to identify the
　　　　　　　　　　　M　　　　S　　　V　　to do
challenges of alternative work styles that companies and workers
　　　　　　　　　　　　　　　　関係代名詞のthat
will have to cope with in the future.

「コワーキング」は、全然違う新しい働き方だ。マンション内のコワーキングスペースは、ホームオフィスのようなくつろいだ雰囲気とリラックスしたコーヒーラウンジの環境をあわせたものだ。コワーカーたちは、マンションに個人用デスクを借りて、会議室、オフィスの備品、そしてラウンジのスペースのような共有スペースをシェアする。「コワーキング」は、一部の在宅勤務者にとって、孤立感や孤独感を解消する助けとなる可能性がある。

　一方で、家で仕事をしたり、他の新しい働き方を実践したりすることは、いつも完璧な解決策となるとは限らない。労働者の中には、雇用者の期待に応えようと、がんばりすぎる者もいるかもしれない。このせいで、ストレス過多や過労につながる可能性がある。新しい仕事の関係者と会うことがより限られていて、もっと孤独を感じる労働者もいる。従来のオフィスは、仕事上の環境であるだけでなく、人と交わる重要な環境でもある。労働者の中には、従来のオフィスで仕事をすることを、人付き合いのうえでより快適に感じる人もいる。うまくいけば、より多くの研究が、企業や労働者が将来対処すべき、新しい働き方が持つ課題を特定するための手助けとなるだろう。

1 環境
2 社会
3 環境
4 健康
5 IT・テクノロジー
6 医学
7 環境
8 IT・テクノロジー
9 教育
10 社会

語 彙 リ ス ト

informal	形	くつろいだ
atmosphere	名	雰囲気
relaxed	形	くつろいだ
private	形	個人の
equipment	名	備品
solve	動	解決する
isolation	名	孤立
loneliness	名	孤独
on the other hand	熟	一方で
solution	名	解決策

meet one's expectations	熟	～の期待に応える
result in	熟	～という結果になる
overwork	名	過労
contact	名	つて（関係者）
limited	形	限られている
social	形	社交の
comfortable	形	快適な
hopefully	副	うまくいけば
identify	動	特定する
cope with	熟	対処する

▶ 単語10回CHECK　1　2　3　4　5　6　7　8　9　10

Recently, alternative work styles are giving workers the opportunity to work in totally different environments. Imagine making a cup of coffee in your kitchen and starting to work by turning on your computer in your office at home. This recent trend is called "telecommuting" or "teleworking." Some companies have closed their offices and all of their employees and managers are telecommuting. Other companies have assigned certain employees to work in this way. Telecommuting eliminates the rush hour commute for workers and saves companies thousands of dollars in rent and utilities for office space. Will more companies consider working at home or other alternative work styles? Does this mean that the traditional work style will fade away in the future? A number of companies are using a combination of traditional and alternative work styles. Many workers and companies are looking for more flexibility to help make their work and personal lives more convenient, efficient and productive. Some companies claim that alternative work styles lead to higher productivity. These new working styles are already being practiced in many technology companies.

Alternative work styles are increasing in popularity because the technology supports a more mobile working style. However, workers spend about 40 years of their lives in jobs, so the work environment is an important concern. This trend has created other alternative working styles including "open seating" or "hotdesking," "officing," "hoteling," and "co-working." "Open seating" or "hotdesking" is a system where workers do not have assigned desks. They come into the office and sit at a group of desks on a first-come, first-served basis. Another similar concept is mobile desks or "officing." Mobile desks can be moved into different arrangements for individual work or teamwork. These also have proven to be efficient for workers and financially rewarding for companies.

Moreover, alternative work styles can also include relocating to other work spaces. "Hoteling" can be used for consultants or other freelance groups that only need office space for a short period. Seating at desks in the office is arranged by the company only when needed. "Co-working" is a very different alternative work style. Co-working spaces in apartment buildings combine the informal atmosphere of the home office with a relaxed coffee lounge environment. Co-workers rent a private desk in the apartment and share the common areas, which may include meeting areas, office equipment and lounge space. "Co-working" can help solve feelings of isolation and loneliness for some telecommuters.

On the other hand, working at home or in other alternative work styles is not always the perfect solution. Some workers may try too hard to meet their employer's expectations. This could result in increased stress and overwork. Meeting new business contacts is more limited, and some workers feel more isolated. The traditional office is not only a business environment but also an important social environment. Some workers feel more comfortable socially in a traditional office. Hopefully, more research will help to identify the challenges of alternative work styles that companies and workers will have to cope with in the future.

BACKGROUND KNOWLEDGE

survival of the fittest

　ちょうど本書を書いている期間にも、新型コロナウイルスの感染拡大により、私たちの働き方に大きな変化が起こりました。多くの企業が積極的にリモートワークを取り入れることで、**通勤時間帯の混雑を解消し、オフィス内での社員の交流を減らすこと**で、**ウイルスの蔓延を抑えるのに多大な貢献**をしています。

　私自身も、年間に複数回行っていた講演会が中止になり、まったく東京から出ない生活になりました。編集者の方々との打ち合わせも、テレビ会議になり、最低限の打ち合わせや、授業の撮影以外は、外出を控える生活となりました。

　無理だと思っていた在宅での仕事も、多少の適応の難しさはあったにせよ、今では当たり前のようにこなしています。ウイルスの感染の危険性を減らして、在宅でできる仕事を増やした結果生まれたのが、この『**ソリューションシリーズ**』でもあります。

　改めて、**重要なのは適応力**であり、**その場その場に応じて、自分を変えられる対応力**だと痛感する日々です。最後に、『進化論』で有名なチャールズ・ダーウィンの格言をご覧ください。私自身、常に大切にしている格言の1つです。

It is not the strongest of the species that survives, nor the most intelligent that survives. It is the one that is most adaptable to change.
生き残る種とは、最も強いものでも、最も知的なものでもない。それは、変化に最もよく適応したものである。

　It is not A that ～, nor A′ that ～. で「**～なのはAでもA′でもない**」という**強調構文**です。第2文のItは「生き残る種」を指しており、thatは関係代名詞、それ以下がthe oneを修飾しています。

　タイトルの *survival of the fittest* は、日本語に直すと「**適者生存**」となります。

　「**生き残るのは、強いものではない。変化に適応したものだ**」、これを肝に銘じて、**新しい世界や変化することを積極的に取り入れることで、未来は開けてくるもの**だと思います。

おわりに

　本書を最後まで読んでくださった読者の方一人一人に、心より御礼申し上げます。本書は、この本の前身となる『**大学入試　レベル別英語長文問題ソリューション**』の音読がしやすい短めの語数の長文を揃えるという特長を維持しつつ、さらに**扱うテーマを最新のものに厳選**することで、**志望校の過去問演習に入る直前の1冊**をイメージして執筆しました。

　試験本番の1週間前でも終われるように、問題数をあえて10題に限定しています。

　問題を解いて**解説を読んで終わりの長文の勉強は、終わりにしましょう。**重要なのは、**1つの長文を自分のものにして先に進むこと、出てきた単語を必ず覚えて、10回音読すること**です。必要なのは、**皆さんの能動的な姿勢**です。

　本書はまだスタンダードレベルという基本的なレベルなので、本書の10の英文を完璧にしたら、ぜひ次のハイレベルへと進んでください。ハイレベルにおいても、**音読に最適な最新テーマの良問を10題**揃えています。本シリーズが、あなたの人生を変えるシリーズとなることを願っています。

　最後に、本書の企画・編集を担当してくださった（株）かんき出版の前澤美恵子様、本書に素敵なデザインを施してくださったワーク・ワンダースの鈴木智則様、本書の校正を念入りにしてくださった（株）オルタナプロの渋谷超様やその他の先生方、『ソリューション最新テーマ編』シリーズのアイディアを授けてくださった中森泰樹先生、最後までお付き合いいただいた読者の皆様に、心から御礼申しあげます。

肘井　学

【著者紹介】

肘井 学（ひじい・がく）

●──慶應義塾大学文学部英米文学専攻卒業。全国のさまざまな予備校をへて、リクルートが主催するネット講義サービス「スタディサプリ」で教鞭をとり、高校生、受験生から英語を学びなおす社会人まで、圧倒的な満足度を誇る。

●──「スタディサプリ」で公開される「英文読解」の講座は、年間25万人の生徒が受講する超人気講座となっている。さらに「東大英語」「京大英語」を担当し、受講者に多くの成功体験を与えている。

●──週刊英和新聞「朝日ウィークリー（Asahi Weekly）」にてコラムを連載するなど、幅広く活躍中。

●──著書に『大学入試 肘井学の読解のための英文法が面白いほどわかる本』『大学入試 肘井学の ゼロから英語長文が面白いほどわかる本』『大学入試 ゼロから英文法が面白いほどわかる本』『大学入試 肘井学の 作文のための英文法が面白いほどわかる本』（KADOKAWA）、『大学入試 すぐわかる英文法』『大学入試 すぐ書ける自由英作文』『大学入試 絶対できる英語リスニング』（教学社）、『高校の英文法が1冊でしっかりわかる本』『高校の英文読解が1冊でしっかりわかる本』（かんき出版）などがある。

だいがくにゅうし べつえい ごちょうぶんもんだい さいしん へん
大学入試 レベル別英語長文問題ソリューション最新テーマ編1　スタンダードレベル

2021年11月1日　　第1刷発行
2023年11月20日　　第5刷発行

著　者──肘井　学
発行者──齊藤　龍男
発行所──株式会社かんき出版
　　　　　東京都千代田区麹町4-1-4　西脇ビル　〒102-0083
　　　　　電話　営業部：03（3262）8011代　編集部：03（3262）8012代
　　　　　FAX　03（3234）4421　　　　　　　振替　00100-2-62304
　　　　　https://kanki-pub.co.jp/
印刷所──大日本印刷株式会社